CW01018488

JUST A BOY

Kevin P. Bourke

MINERVA PRESS
ATLANTA LONDON SYDNEY

JUST A BOY
Copyright © Kevin P. Bourke 1999

All Rights Reserved

ISBN 0 75410 542 3

First Published 1999 by
MINERVA PRESS
315–317 Regents Street
London W1R 7YB

Printed in Great Britain for Minerva Press

JUST A BOY

To my Grandfather,
Seamus De'Burca
Who's patience got this through.
And Gary Maguire.
Tickadeboo!

Chapter One

Today was May 20th, and like every other school leaver I was happy, for my schooldays were over. And yet in some part of me I was sad, for my childhood days had almost come to an end. As the school bus pulled away we all cheered. If we had expressed what we felt deep down, it should have been tears, but then what can you expect from a bus full of boys? I was to become a pupil at the National Sea Training School and on the Tuesday just after the bank holiday, I kissed my mother goodbye and set off for the railway station. I caught the eight-thirty train, and as I climbed aboard, I looked at all the people with long faces, ready to start a new day.

The train moved from station to station, and all I had on my mind was the Sea School. Soon we pulled into Gravesend Central. I picked up my bag, opened the door and stepped on to the platform. It was raining and quite cold. I walked towards the ticket collector with my ticket ready in one hand and my bag in the other. I was to stay outside the station and wait for a blue transit van with the school's name on its side.

The rain did not stop, and I was shivering with the cold in my shoes. The van was now fifteen minutes late, and by this time another five boys with bags had gathered around the area in which I was standing.

Eventually the van arrived and an old man in a black uniform got out. 'Are you all for the Sea School?' he asked.

'Yes,' we replied.

'Right, throw your bags in the back of the van and jump in.'

We all hesitated as to who would get in first. Then I threw my bag in and got in myself; the rest followed.

'You all in?' the man shouted. He started up the engine and we set off for the Sea School.

I looked out of the window, the rain had stopped and a rainbow was forming in the sky. A couple of the boys were now talking, opposite me sat one who looked very upset. I might upset him even more if I speak to him, I thought, but I'll have to speak to him sooner or later, and get to know him because I'm going to be living with this lad for the next three months.

I uttered my first words: 'Oh well, we're nearly there.'

He smiled. Then we started chatting. His name was Neil Walters, a tall lad from Stoke-on-Trent in Staffordshire. He told me he was upset because he had left his girlfriend behind that morning.

'She was in tears when I said goodbye,' he said.

As we all got into our somewhat limited conversations, one of the lads spotted the school in the distance. Silence crept among us as we got nearer. I became, very nervous just wondering what it was going to be like. The van pulled up.

'Right then, here we are,' said the driver. I made sure I wasn't as eager to get out as I had been to get in. Finally though we all climbed down from the van, and followed the driver.

We walked through a small foyer and came to the registrar's office. We went inside and sat down. It was a very big room with desks. There were several other boys being seen to, who had arrived earlier. As I waited, I took out my birth certificate and insurance cards, which I would have to give to the registrar. My turn came and I sat down at the desk handing over my birth certificate and insurance cards. The registrar asked if I would like to leave any valuables or money for safe keeping. Well, I didn't have any valuables except my watch, which I wore all the time and as for money, I had thirteen pounds; I gave him eight for the time being.

Outside, it had started to rain once more. It made me very cold and isolated as I sat and waited for the others, I was thinking ahead to when the training would be over and I'd go to sea. A tall officer with a moustache was calling me. 'Come on laddie,' he said, 'you're not in bed now.'

'Sorry, I was just thinking,' I said. The rest of the boys had finished with the registrar, so we left the office and went down a very long corridor. The tall officer's name was Jacobs – a neat military fanatic, who always went by the book; he took us upstairs to the library, where the rest of the boys, who had arrived earlier were waiting and making a right racket!

'All right, shut your noise.' There wasn't a sound. Jacobs, had spoken. We all sat down and he began to speak in a very persuasive manner.

'You're going to love it here, aren't you lads? Well?' he said.

'Yes, Sir,' we replied.

He gave each boy a padlock and key for a locker. Then a boy in a black uniform came in and approached Jacobs.

'Right, you lot,' he said, 'you are now J Class and you will occupy dormitory nine, and this lad here is senior leading hand Phillips. He is wearing the school uniform; this is the School's number one uniform, which you will wear *only* when you go outside the school, and on special occasions. Now, I want you all to go along with Phillips and he will show you your dormitory, and I'm sure he will answer any questions you may have. By the look of you, you could all do with a haircut, so you are all obliged to be standing outside the barber's shop in half an hour. Is that clear? Right, I'll see you then.'

We went across the courtyard and up the stairs, finally arriving at dormitory nine. Each of the padlocks we had been given had a number. The number on my padlock was five and so that was my locker number. It was right opposite my door. There was also a bunk bed, and luckily enough mine was the top one. We threw our bags in the lockers and started asking Phillips questions, like, 'What's the grub like?' and 'how short does the barber cut hair?'

'Well,' he said, 'the grub is okay and as for Sweeney, well, you'll meet up with him in a minute.'

The school had a somewhat public school resemblance, a sort of modern Tom Brown's School days; everyone was known by surname, and what with the short hair and uniforms, this was the exact image. Well, after being scalped by Sweeney, my head soon felt the cold, and as for my stomach, I was starving. We made our way to the mess hall to sample the grub. Ever since that morning when we arrived, the senior boys had great pleasure in calling us the new lads – Peanuts. I wondered if they had forgot to add the KP.

That evening we all received our first bedding. This was an hour before lights outs, which was at ten-thirty. Later on that night, I started talking to a Tom Murphy. We chatted away for most of the night. He too, was from Stoke-on-Trent. I started talking about a film I had seen. It was called *The Exorcist* and I had Murphy hiding under the covers as I told him about it. Being new boys – Peanuts – we didn't quite grasp the rules at first, because after 'lights out' we were not to make a sound, unless it was to snore! Both Murphy and I were told to be quiet by a patrolling leading hand. The next day we all went down to collect our uniforms, which were either too small or too large. I'm sure the man who measured my waist left his hand inside the tape measure giving me an extra four inches.

With our uniforms on and the weeks going by, we soon blended in with the school. We had plenty of fun and laughs during the first four weeks. We all took two tests on fire-fighting and life boats. I managed to pass the fire-fighting test but failed the life boats. Poor old Murphy failed both. As we weren't old enough to go out to the local public house, we made do with the school's youth club, which was just outside the grounds. The club had various amusements like darts, snooker and a big television room. It also had a snack bar with all the essentials a spotty sixteen-year-old could lick his lips for. We all enjoyed ourselves in the club from six until nine-thirty when they had to close, but most of the lads only went there for a decent crap, as the toilets there had locked doors, dirty magazines and soft toilet paper.

*

There were times at weekends when you could go home on leave. It was a release on a Friday afternoon just to get back into civilian clothes. You felt yourself again; and it was great to get home and go out with your mates. You could stay out as long as you liked, knowing you could stay in bed the following day. On Sunday, what better than a real roast dinner done by Mum, whose cooking one appreciates when one has been away.

But that's the only thing I liked about Sundays. Other than the roast dinner, I loathed Sundays; always very quiet and dismal. Then came the dreaded Monday morning, on which I made my way back to school. With school in sight, at the end of the very long road, a car pulled up. It was one of the officers, Mr Relf.

'You want a lift?' he said.

My legs answered that question.

'Enjoyed your leave?' he asked.

'Yes, it was fine.'

I was just on time as we pulled in to the car park; I quickly jumped out and thanked him.

'That's okay,' he said.

I ran quickly to my dormitory, where all the other boys were dressed and ready to go down for muster – all except Murphy who hadn't even arrived. He had gone home to Stoke-on-Trent, as that Saturday his sister had got married. I quickly got into my working gear, and while I was buttoning up my jacket, I looked through the window, and in the distance, running, with a huge case, I saw Murphy, who was by now already late.

I ran down the stairs and quickly got into my line for muster. The inspection began. It was one of those dismal Monday mornings. There was a lot of talking among the lines. Then a huge voice echoed all over the court. It was Jacobs.

'Shut your noise and stand easy.'

There was silence, just as if All Mighty God had spoken. Then, all of a sudden, like a mighty flash Murphy ran round the corner, almost knocking one of the officers over.

'Sorry I'm late,' he explained, 'I missed the train.'

There was laughter everywhere, and the voice of Jacobs ordering us to be quiet; just the thing to brighten up a Monday morning, but not for poor old Murphy who made the blunder, for he received two hours' detention!

Then we all went to our classes, and that week we started our catering training to become stewards, observing the golden rule of cleanliness, how to make a proper bunk and the correct way to lay a table. I didn't know why they taught us all that, for I thought that when we went to sea, all we'd be doing was washing dishes and scrubbing the decks.

This week our teacher was a Mr Annetts. 'Good morning, class!' he said.

'Good morning, Sir,' we all replied.

Annetts was a practical joker, but when Murphy, who had already had the whole school in hysterics, came into the classroom, he and he alone made us all laugh – especially me! I couldn't control myself and nor for that matter could Murphy.

'Leave the room!'

Both Murphy and myself were ordered out. While shutting the door behind us still laughing, we noticed the chief catering officer, Mr Plumb, coming up the stairs.

'Bloody hell, Murphy! We're in for it now.'

Murphy quickly spotted a mop and a bucket of water standing outside a cleaning cupboard. 'You get the mop out and I'll get the polish,' said Murphy. We both took off our jackets and threw water over our foreheads. Murphy was soon hard at work on his hands and knees, while I mopped the floor like I'd never mopped before.

Mr Plumb passed us and said, 'Well done, lads. Keep it up.'

'Yes Sir, thank you Sir.'

He went, right past Mr Annetts' classroom and up the next flight of stairs. Murphy and I were relieved.

'Thank Christ for that. Better we had done that, Kev eh, than stand there like dummies? He would definitely have asked us what we were doing.'

'Yeah, you're right! Good thinking: the mop and polish.'

We quickly put the items, which had just saved our necks back in the cupboard. Then Annetts' classroom door opened and we all went out for a break.

*

After lunch that day, we had a lesson called a 'Doeby' which meant it was washing day. We mainly washed our jeans and tee shirts, not forgetting the smelly socks and dirty skiddies. We had Annetts for that lesson, which meant Murphy and I facing him once again. It wasn't a pleasant reunion, for he gave Murphy and me a hard time that afternoon; we were last at getting our gear washed and dried, and last on the ironing board.

In front of us on the ironing board were two lads Murph and myself didn't like, McGee and Procter. Both were in our dormitory and both of them were mouthy. Murph was trying to hurry them along, as there was only ten minutes left of the lesson. McGee was ironing a shirt and chatting away to Procter at the same time. He sounded just like an old hen.

'Hurry up, McGee,' I said, 'there's only ten minutes left and we would like to use the iron as well.'

'Whose fault is that? You shouldn't laugh so much in class, should you?'

He sounded just like a bloody schoolgirl who always tells the teacher. Just then, McGee's shirt, which was nylon, slid off the table.

'I saw that,' he said. 'You pushed that on purpose. I'll see you later in the dormitory, Bourke.'

'That's fine with me McGee.'

'Lovely,' Murph said. 'You can have McGee and I'll deal with Procter.'

That evening, we both went up to the club for a game of darts, but, trust our luck, McGee and Procter were playing. I felt like using McGee's face as the dartboard. No, I thought, I'll control my temper until later. We went into the television room; there was a film on, so we sank into armchairs and with a coke and a burger – the only decent grub you get round here – we watched the corny Western. Bored to death by this we decided to go and have a game of pool.

There was only one pool tables and, believe it or not, McGee and Procter had had the same idea and got there before us.

'Sorry, we beat you to it.'

It was nearly nine so we both decided to go back to the dormitory and get ready for them to return.

While back in the dormitory, I was helping Murph finish off a letter to one of his girlfriends. Then I noticed McGee and Procter coming along the road. 'Look Murph, they're coming.'

'Good, lets get ready for them.'

We hid round by their bunks. We could hear them coming up the stairs, both of them laughing and saying what they were going to do to us. They entered the dormitory.

'Where are you then, Bourke?' said McGee. 'I'm ready for you; we are not scared, are you?'

I came out of my hiding place, along with Murphy. 'No, McGee, I'm not scared of you.'

The dormitory was empty except for the four us. Then McGee dived at me, but I just jumped out of his way. Poor McGee lay on the floor, helpless. I let him stand up and then I hit him quite a few times on the head and body. He dropped his head and hit me in the stomach, but he was weakening. So I brought my knees up and hit him right under the chin. Poor McGee was on his back again, his nose bleeding.

'No more, Bourke, I've had enough,' he said.

Murphy dealt with Procter easily enough, and after that incident the two of them kept well clear of both of us.

*

At the end of our catering exam, both Murph and myself passed. We felt pretty glad for there were only a couple of weeks left, and then Murph and I were to go our separate ways. The next week there was a sports day at the school, and parents and friends could come as spectators. During the week spent preparing for the sports, all we had for the whole week were films, mainly about safety on board ship.

Soon it was the eve of the sports day – Murphy had entered for several races. Unfortunately, I was only in one – the sprint race. Murph was also in the sprints so we had a wager on to see who would win.

'Saturday, 28th July, 1974. It's sports day here at the Sea School,' shouted the speaker. It was a hot and very sunny day. My family had come down to see me. Then the speaker announced the start of the sprint race. There were ten runners in all, including Murphy and myself. The starter called us to the line.

'Take your marks, get set,' and then he fired the gun.

We were off, and all ten of us were out to win. Alas! I crossed the line but didn't win; neither did Murphy. I suppose I didn't do to badly out of ten, I came third, while Murphy came fourth. So I won the bet.

The boy who won was a Scot and a flying Scot at that. His name was Jimmy. Both Murphy and Jimmy met my family after the race, but fourth place was not good enough for Murphy. He entered another four races and won them all! He was highly rewarded afterwards at the prize-giving. As I came third I received a fountain pen and matching cuff links. Murphy received an electric drill, a foodmixer, an electric blanket and an electric razor. The sports day came to an end, Murphy being the sensation of the afternoon. I didn't even get a chance of meeting the Murph family he was so busy winning races. All the spectators left after an enjoyable day at the school. Then we had to clean the rubbish; as they say, get the place shipshape.

After the hectic but enjoyable sports day it was back to the old routine. But for Murph and me there were only five days left, for now we were finally the senior boys of the school, although we weren't leading hands, as we weren't spoken highly of by the officers. McGee and Procter were, but that didn't bother us, for a friend of ours, Steve Snow, was the senior leading hand of the catering department, and he made sure that McGee and Procter didn't step out of line.

The days dragged by like months but it was finally the eve of our departure from the school. We were all warned by Mr Plumb, the chief catering officer, that if we were to cause any trouble that night we would have to stay at the school for another week. While he said that, he had a beady eye on Murphy and me.

But we didn't listen to him, for the leading hand in our dormitory was a boy who looked just like a lion but when he roared he sounded more like a mouse. Murphy knew that no one could keep him in his bunk that night not even leading hand Denton. It was a night for celebration and Murphy was out to celebrate.

'Oh come on, Murphy, there's a good chap, please get back into bed,' Denton begged. We pulled lion, as he was known to himself and others – but not to Murph or me – out of his bunk and on to the floor where I gagged him and threw all his bedding over him, while Murphy, courageous as he was, went downstairs where he had hidden the loudspeaker which was used for sports day, under the staircase, borrowing it just for that night. He climbed over the railings and went into the courtyard. That's when Murphy had his little say.

'Wakey, wakey, Peanuts, this is the captain speaking. The ship is sinking, everyone overboard!'

Every dormitory light was on, and the night officer put all the courtyard lights on too, but all that could be seen was a loudspeaker left sitting on the ground. I ungaged Denton and told him not to mention a word to anyone. Murphy was now in his bunk fast asleep. There was a dormitory check by the night officer and the leading hands, but most of us were asleep, especially Murphy who didn't even wake up!

'Hurray!' was the first sound that morning, and that was made by Murphy. We all washed, packed and took our bedding down. We were to receive our discharge books, identity cards and other documents. Then we all climbed aboard the bus and made our exit *en route* for home. Murph and I exchanged addresses and phone numbers and swore we would see each other again.

At the station, we all said our farewells, and I was to get on a different train to Murphy. As my train pulled out I waved goodbye and wondered if I was waving farewell and 'See you soon!' Their figures got smaller, until I could no longer see them. I shut the window and sat down. I was all alone, with a short journey home.

*

I must have fallen asleep on the way, for when I woke up, the train was standing at my station as if it were waiting for me to get off so that it could be on its way. I walked along the platform, still half asleep. I gave the ticket collector my ticket and made my way out of the station. I started to walk, but I was really knackered. It was over a mile to my house, so I got a taxi, and still regret it. It cost me a pound and it's not even a mile, and he was sure of a tip. 'No chance,' I said, 'it's daylight robbery,' and I slammed the door.

My mother came out to greet me.

'It is nice to be home again,' I said, while drinking a glass of cold orange juice.

They were all getting ready for their summer holidays. I couldn't go, as I had to wait for a ship. I was watching television in the front room, but was interrupted by a telephone call. It was the Shipping Federation, offering me a ship for the Monday morning. The bloke at the other end called the ship the *Jarvis Bay*. I said, 'Okay, I'll take it,' and said goodbye.

When I told my father the name of the ship, he said, 'It can't be; the *Jarvis Bay* was sunk during the war.'

'So it's a ghost ship,' a wisecrack, from a very funny brother.

'Well I'll find out on Monday.'

I had an early night, as I had got up at the crack of dawn that morning. I said goodbye to them before I went to bed as they were all to leave very early the next day. They must have been as quiet as mice because any little noise wakes me.

It was about ten-thirty when I eventually got out of bed. It was a very hot day, so I poured myself a glass of cold orange juice and sat in one of the deck chairs in the garden. Even the cat was too hot. She was asleep in the shade of our plum tree.

Just then the phone rang. It was my friend Paul Jack, who had just come back from the Bahamas where he had spent a two week holiday, staying with his elder brother who was living out there. 'I meant to phone you last night,' he said.

'I'm glad you didn't,' I replied, 'I had an early night last night, I was dead beat.'

I told him to come around for the weekend and he agreed. I then phoned Dick and Peter. They all arrived that afternoon. Paul brought two hundred duty free cigarettes and a big bottle of Bacardi, which he had bought on the flight over from the Bahamas. As the house was vacant, we decided to have a party. I asked a few more friends too. Paul Reader arrived in his transit van. Well, he needed one; an ordinary car would be too small, for he is well over six feet tall and weighs nearly eighteen stone.

Everyone got drunk that night, especially Pete and a girl called Sandy. Those of us who could still walk straight helped the pair of them off with their clothes and put them into one of the single beds. There were ten of us in all, and using the sofa and the armchairs, everyone got a good night's sleep, or shall I say a good morning's sleep. Most of us didn't turn the lights out until way past six on Sunday morning.

That afternoon we all started to stagger out for role call. Well that's what it sounded like. Paul Jack and Dick were taking a bath together. They were still drunk, and trying to sing with the radio blaring away. The sound or rather the racket, woke the hungry Paul Reader.

'Right, what's for breakfast then?'

Nobody else was hungry, except for Pete, who was still eating peanuts and drinking brown ale.

In the kitchen, two of the girls, Jill and Jackie, were doing bacon and eggs, mainly for Paul Reader's benefit, although this could not fill the big appetite. He was quickly rooting through the larder, but nothing caught his eye. 'I fancy a roast dinner,' he said. He was quickly out of the front door, with Pete right behind him. We heard the van take off, as if he were in a Grand Prix.

By this time, Paul and Dick had fallen asleep in the bath and Sandy, Linda and Deb were still in bed; nor could I blame them, for the whole place looked as if a bomb had hit it. Jill was trying to find her bra and Jackie her tights; and outside I could hear Paul's van pull up, then the two of them banging at the front door. It was a sight for greedy bellies alone; for Paul had a huge piece of meat under his arm. It was a leg of lamb and it was for our Sunday lunch.

Paul was looking for a dish big enough while Paul, Jack and Dick were now awake and out of the bath. They all stood in the hallway staring at the huge leg of lamb, still dripping wet.

I said, 'There is only one dish big enough and that's only brought out at Christmas for the turkey,' but my belly was empty too so I got the dish down from the larder and it was a perfect fit. The leg of lamb just about got itself into the dish. Jackie quickly peeled some potatoes and put them in too and then the whole lot was put in the oven. A couple of us prepared some vegetables and put them on the stove.

While the rest of us were trying to tidy up, Paul Reader was laying the table; but as well as laying the table he was looking for a plate big enough to hold his dinner. Just before dinner was ready, Jill and myself went up to the off-licence to get a couple of bottles of wine, which I thought would go down very nicely. When we returned, the feast began. With the ten large plates around the small table, Paul started to carve the meat. I served the wine after the huge dinner, and our stomachs couldn't say no to a nice rest in the sitting-room. Even big Paul had eaten quite enough.

After lounging around for a couple of hours, and with the washing up all done, we all decided to go out for a drive in Paul's van. It was about seven in the evening and still quite light outside. We ended up in a country pub called The Fox and Hounds – just the thing to end a beautiful day.

I was the first to be dropped off that evening. They all said goodbye and all wished me luck. Then they went on their way. The house had already been cleaned that afternoon. It was all nice and tidy; but it was very quiet. Before I turned in, I packed my bag for the next day making sure I left my discharge book and papers on the table so I would not forget them.

I had a restless night. I just couldn't get to sleep. All I had on my mind was the following day and the ship. I wondered where the ship would go and how long it would be away. I set my mind on some remote desert island, with swaying palm trees and beautiful girls in grass skirts, and me walking along the beach with its golden sands beneath my feet, gazing out at the deep blue sea and slowly I dozed off.

Chapter Two

I remember awakening to a screaming alarm clock, telling me it was time to get up! I'm sure it woke the whole street. I slowly got out from beneath the warm sheets and made my way towards the bathroom. I stared into the mirror and felt like going back to bed. But after a cold wash and a good clean-up, I soon felt my proper self. I made some toast and poured out a glass of orange. I turned on the radio to hear the cheerful voice of Tony Blackburn. He made me feel a bit better but with those corny jokes of his he usually makes me cry. I noticed the time and had to hurry. I turned off Tony Blackburn and phoned for a taxi to take me to the station. I put my jacket on and put my discharge book and my papers in the inside pocket. Then I opened the door. The taxi had just arrived, so I picked up my bag, said goodbye to the cat, went outside and got into the taxi. As the taxi pulled away, I took one glance at my home, then I turned around and sat back in the seat.

The taxi soon arrived at the station. I grabbed my bag, paid the driver, went into the station and bought my ticket. The platform was empty. The train arrived early and I climbed aboard an empty carriage. Well, I thought it was empty. On the way, I started to sing aloud, but little did I notice the little old lady who was sitting behind me. She got off the train at the stop before mine, gave me a very funny look and then slammed the door. I felt a bit embarrassed – but I also had a little laugh.

The train soon came to my stop and I could see the Federation just across the road. I climbed down and handed the collector my ticket. Crossing the busy road I went inside the building and up to the desk.

'Good morning, I was told to come in today to join a ship called the *Jarvis Bay*,' I said.

'Oh yes, you must be Kevin Bourke and don't you mean the *Jervis Bay*? That, was probably my fault.'

'Yes, but where is it going?' I asked.

'Well, nowhere at the moment. It leaves for Australia in ten days time.' He then asked for my discharge book and union card. On the board in the office I noticed the words *Jervis Bay*, Australia 18th August, 1974, One Catering Boy.

As soon as I read it, the bloke to whom I gave my papers was rubbing it off. Oh no, I thought, the ship has sailed without me.

'Why are you rubbing it off?' I asked.

'Because you're it; the ship wanted a catering boy and you're it.'

'Oh, I didn't know. I suppose there's a lot I've got to get used to.'

'Right,' he said, 'here are your papers. Now go and sit down over there and a bloke will come for you to take you on board.'

No sooner had I sat down, than an old man poked his head around the door. 'The lad for *Jervis Bay*?'

'Yes,' I said, 'that's me.' I picked up my bag and followed him outside.

'Right, jump in the van.'

'Why the van?' I asked, 'is the ship too far to walk to?'

'Yes,' he said, 'the ship is on the other side of the docks.'

We soon arrived at the ship; he dropped me off at the gangway and then drove off. I was stranded all alone in front of a huge ship. I picked up my bag and started to climb the mighty gangway.

I eventually reached the top, where I was greeted by an

old grumpy sailor. 'What do you want?' he asked.

I hesitated.

'Well, don't keep me here all day. What d'ya want?'

I shyly told him that I was the new catering boy.

'You want the chief steward,' he said. 'Come on, follow me.'

I followed him. As we went inside the ship, it was very dark and very narrow. We went up a flight of stairs and arrived at a door with the number nineteen on it. Above that were the words, 'Chief Steward's Cabin'. He knocked on the door twice but there was no answer.

'He must be ashore,' said the old sailor. 'Oh, well, I'd better take you down to the galley to see the chief cook.'

We went down the flight of stairs and along the corridor. We passed the crew bar, where the old sailor stopped and told the lads in the bar that he wouldn't be long. He was obviously a drinker. Then we came to the galley.

'Cook, Cook,' cried the old sailor.

'Yes, what is it?' replied a voice.

'I've got a young lad here who says he's the new catering boy.'

'Oh, let me look at him.'

A tall cook appeared in front of me.

'Hello lovely, and what's your name?'

I thought, just my bloody luck, a bloody poof for a boss.

The old sailor then left for the bar.

'Well, what's your name?' asked the cook.

'Kevin Bourke,' I replied.

'Oh, lovely. Suits you down to a tee, especially with all that red hair and freckles. Right, follow me and I'll show you your new cabin.'

We went down a flight of stairs and then came to my cabin-to-be. It had the words, 'Catering Boy' on the door.

The cook opened the door and put the light on.

'Isn't it lovely? There's a nice double bed and you have a

washbasin. And if you ever need anything, I'm right next door.'

Bloody marvellous, I thought, a queer boss to work with and living right next door. I threw my bag down and lay on the bed. It was quite a nice cabin. Then there was a knock on the door. It was the Queen again.

'I'm just going to the bar. Why don't you come up in a minute and get to know the lads?'

'Yes, I'll probably pop up there in a minute,' I said.

About ten minutes later, I went to the bar. The big dancing Queen was there, as large as life. He told the whole bar who I was. Then he brought me beer and gave me some cigarettes as I didn't have any.

The bar was packed. The old sailor was in there, downing whisky by the glass. I asked the cook what his name was. At this he told the whole bar.

'Did you hear that, lads? Young Kevin here would like to know my name.'

Everyone listened to the cook.

'My name, deary, is Hilary, if you must know, and I eat little boys like you for breakfast.'

At this the whole bar laughed.

'And if you are a good boy, I'll let you sleep with me homeward bound; but only if you're a good boy!'

The bar was in hysterics. I quickly drank my beer, put the cigarettes in my pocket and went to the door. Hilary was sitting on the lap of one of the deckhand's with his arms around the sailor's neck. Hilary noticed me at the door.

'Oh, you're not going yet, are you?' he said.

At that I replied, 'Hilary, you said something about sleeping with you homeward bound.'

'Yes,' said Hilary, 'only if you're a good boy.'

So I plucked up courage and said, 'I'd rather sleep with Guy the Gorilla.' At that I ran out of the bar and along the corridor, hearing the sound of roaring laughter coming from the bar. Quickly I ran down the stairs and into my cabin, locking the door behind me. There, I picked up my bag and made for the gangway, avoiding the route past the bar.

I reached the gangway, safe and sound, and as fast as my legs would carry me. I ran quickly down, with the thought of the screaming Hilary behind me. I got to the bottom and ran along the road. No wonder the ship needed a new catering boy! Hilary, probably ate the last one.

I started to thumb a lift to the main gate and the first car that came along, stopped.

'Where are you going?' the man asked.

'To the main gate, then the station,' I said.

'Okay, jump in, I'm going that way myself.'

I told him that I'd just been paid off the *Jervis Bay* and was going on leave. I didn't mention anything about leaving because of Hilary. We soon arrived at the main gate, but the guard just waved us on. 'Have you got a pass for that bag of yours?' he said.

'Why, no! Should I have one?'

'Core, you lucky devil,' he said, 'if that guard had looked in the car and seen you didn't have a pass for your bag, he would have made you go back to the ship and get one.'

He pulled up at the station.

'Thanks for the lift,' I said.

'That's okay boy.'

Thank Christ that guard didn't come over. I would have had to face Hilary, once more. Slowly the train pulled out of the station; it moved swiftly down the tracks. Farther and farther I went away from the *Jervis Bay* and Hilary. The train had now picked up speed and I was well on my way.

I was silly really, leaving over a stupid thing like that, because wherever you go, you'll meet up with people like that. But surely not as bad as Hilary? I was now trying to think of what to say when I got home and how I would explain it all to the Shipping Federation.

★

I arrived home to an empty house, for my family were still on holiday. So I phoned one of my friends, Peter. All the others were round his place; they were all still on holidays.

'I thought you had gone to join the ship,' he said.

'Yes, that's what I intended to do this morning – and I did. But I didn't like it or it didn't like me.'

'We'll be around in a minute anyway, Kev. I don't know – jumping ship, and your first one at that!'

I didn't think of that. Now Pete had me worried. I wondered if I could get done by the Shipping Federation. About ten minutes later, Paul's van came hurtling around the corner. They all jumped out and started banging on my front door.

I opened the door and they all charged in and started to ask what had happened. One of the girls even asked if the police were after me.

'No, of course they're not. Well, I hope not.'

That week we all just stayed round Paul Reader's house. Just before we left, I finished off a letter to the Shipping Federation and on the way to Paul's place I bought a stamp and posted it. In the letter I told them why I had left the ship and that I needed a couple of weeks to think it over.

We all had a great time that week. We went swimming every day in a nearby stream and then at night, we went to every pub around. But Saturday came too quickly, for my parents were coming home and I would have to tell them all about it.

Paul ran me home in the van. They were all back and amazed at seeing me at the door. I told them all about it.

'So you're not going to sea after all?' my mother said.

'Oh, of course I am.'

There was a letter on the table for me. It was the reply from the Federation. They gave me two weeks unpaid leave and told me to report back to them on 2nd September, which to me was great news.

Maybe I needed a holiday after all the training I had done!

That afternoon, I got a job working in a factory canteen. I was to start on Monday morning and my wages were to be twenty-two pounds a week, which didn't seem too bad at all, although I didn't know I'd have to work with a load of old women. On Monday morning I started my new job, and after ten minutes with all the old women talking, I felt like running out just like I had done on the *Jervis Bay*. But I thought, I can't keep running away from something I don't like. Anyway, I only intended to stay for two weeks, although I didn't tell them that.

My job consisted of making the toast for breakfast and making up salads for lunch and dinner, and on that Friday after quite an easy week, I received my first pay packet from my boss Mrs Lyons, who was a right old bag. She was always shouting at everyone, including me. Usually when you start a job you have to work a week in hand, but I didn't and so, after receiving my wage packet, I went in to see Mrs Lyons.

'Yes,' she said, 'no mistakes with your wages is there?'

'No,' I said, 'I just thought I'd come in and tell you that I'll be leaving next Friday.'

'What,' she said, very loudly, 'but you've only been here a week.'

'Yes, I know. I'm sorry, but I've decided to go back to sea.'

There was I saying that, and I hadn't even been to sea yet! All very nicely she said, 'Back to sea; all right,' and she left it at that.

I was glad to get out of there that evening, even knowing that all I had left to do was five days. Mind you, I thought Mrs Lyons acted very calmly. I thought she would raise the roof. That weekend, I had a great time spending nearly all my wages. Over the weekend I thought of Mrs Lyons and how calm and nice she had been on that Friday afternoon, but I also thought Monday might be different. She might give me a hard time and work my fingers to the bone. But she was nothing like that. She was like a mother to me all that week. I had an easy time, extra-long lunch breaks and all in all I hardly worked.

But there was also a boy called William working there, a right snotty little sod. William was the same age as me, and did more or less the same work, and on that Friday afternoon I did nothing – I couldn't I was so excited about leaving. But William looked at it differently.

'Come on, Mrs Lyons,' he said, 'I'm doing far too much work, while that Kevin is doing nothing.'

So Mrs Lyons called William and me into her office.

'Kevin,' she said, 'William thinks you're not doing enough work, so do you know what I'm going to do?'

'No,' I said.

'Well, William, I'm going to give Kevin his money now, as he is leaving today, and send him home early.'

You ought to have seen William's face. I thanked Mrs Lyons, put on my coat and said goodbye to everyone, except William who was hard at work doing two jobs. Poor old William!

That evening I stayed in and watched television. I'm glad I did now, for there was a telephone call for me. It was Murphy on a ship in Liverpool and he sounded very drunk. He said the ship he was on was going to the West Indies, and that it would leave the next day. I wished him all the best, and said that I hoped to see him in the future and then said goodbye.

I stayed in all over the weekend, thinking very much about Tuesday and what the ship was going to be like. On the Monday, my father and mother went back to work, and my brothers to school, and I was woke up by a phone call. It was another friend of mine, from the Sea School, Steve Snow. He told me he hadn't got a ship yet, and asked if I had got one. I told him that I was to go to the Federation the next day hoping that they would have a ship for me. I told him that Murphy had rung the night before, and that he was on a ship bound for the West Indies, and then I said cheerio. That evening I went out for a farewell drink with my friends. This time I was determined to get a ship, for you can't keep on having farewell send offs and keep coming back, can you? I said goodbye to all of them, and then made my way home, where my mother was kind enough to pack my bags. She also insisted on seeing me off the next day. I said goodbye to my father and brothers, that night as they wouldn't be around when I left the next day.

On Tuesday morning the taxi arrived and my mother had tears in her eyes. I kissed her goodbye, got into the taxi and left. It was a quiet train ride, and I felt very relaxed until I arrived at the Shipping Federation where the head man gave me a rollicking. After receiving a good telling-off, the man behind the desk offered me a ship called the RFA *Green Rover*. This was a small tanker, which refuelled the Royal Navy Ships. The ship was at Chatham in Kent. The man told me it would be away for six months and that it was going to the Far East.

I've always longed to go to the Far East, especially to Hong Kong and Japan. He drew a small map to show me how to get there, I didn't really listen to what he had to say, and just grabbed the small map and said goodbye. I had to get the ferry over to Gravesend, and then I caught a bus to Chatham. The bus was the 35a, and I went upstairs and sat in the back seat. Just for laughs, I pretended to the old bus conductor, that I was a foreigner.

I showed him the small piece of paper with my destination on it. Mind you, I made sure I was no fool with British currency.

The bus conductor, who was very concerned, said, 'You Scandinavian?'

I just shook my head.

'Or German?'

Still I didn't reply.

'Or are you Dutch?' The bewildered bus conductor left me and went downstairs.

I could hear him talking to another person.

'Bloody foreigners!' he said.

After a long and bumpy ride, the bus finally arrived at Chatham.

The Conductor said, 'This is your stop.'

So I went downstairs, looked at the bus conductor, and, still having him on I said, 'Thank-achurn.'

A big smile came over the man's face. 'Are you Deutchlander?' he said.

I replied, 'Wrong, I'm Englander; goodbye!'

The bus pulled away with an astonished bus conductor on it. Yet he had the last laugh, as I had got off at the wrong place. Although the conductor did have the right stop, according to the road sign, the ship was on the other side of the docks; and with a heavy case in my hand, I had a long walk.

Eventually I reached the gate where the ship was berthed. I was stopped at the gate and had to show my identity card to the policeman. He pointed straight ahead at a grey small looking tanker.

'That's the *Green Rover*,' he said.

Well I didn't expect that. Then again, I didn't think it would be green. I went on board, and a man on the gangway asked if I was the new catering boy. I was and he took me down below to the purser's office.

Inside the small, cramped office I met the purser, a bearded man called Davis, and the second steward, who was called White. They both explained to me that the ship would be away for nine months, and not six months as the Federation had told me. They also told me the places which the ship would visit. So I didn't hesitate. I quickly signed the articles. The second steward showed me to my cabin, which, by the way, I had to share. The boy I shared it with was called Dick. He didn't like being called Richard. He was the galley boy and had been at sea for nearly six months. He was a plumpish lad from Birmingham.

After I had unpacked my bags White, the second steward, took me down below to explain to me what my new duties would be – to keep the crew mess clean. From now on I was known as the mess boy, but luckily enough, I didn't have to start in the mess until the next day. While I was looking around the mess room I noticed Dick hard at work in the galley, scrubbing the huge pans. I was relieved that I didn't have to do that job. The only washing up I did was the plates and cutlery.

I also kept a small mess room clean which belonged to the petty officers and was next door to the crew bar. There were only about eight men who used it. Opposite the mess room was the crew bar, which at the time was packed out, as it was break time. I entered the bar, bought a beer, and sat on a stool. Most of the men in the bar were deckhands with a couple of stewards and greasers who worked down below in the engine room.

★

After dinner that evening, I went ashore with one of the stewards, Andy. We went into one of the local pubs, called The Bridge House. Both of us sunk well into the hard stuff, especially Andy – he suffered when he was sober, and when he was drunk you couldn't tell whether he was speaking in English or Dutch. Anyway, he was telling me to watch out for the second cook, called Lenny, who usually threw his weight about.

Long after closing time, both Andy and myself were feeling a bit under. We helped one another to our feet, and made our way back to the ship, singing and dancing in the street. At the gate, the policeman assisted both of us safely to our ship.

Eventually on board, a couple of deckhands helped us to our cabins where no sooner had I shut my eyes, than I was being called for work. It was only five-thirty and all I felt like doing was taking my clothes off and getting into bed.

Dick, who was dressed and ready to go down to start work, was pulling me off my bunk and helping me into my working clothes. At last I was ready, although I didn't know what for. I just felt like sleeping. I made my way down to the crew mess, which to me looked a right state.

I managed to lay the tables for breakfast and cleaned up a bit. It all went quite smoothly that morning, until I bumped into Lenny, the second cook. He was very fat and covered in tattoos. After meeting Lenny every thing went wrong. Just before dinner that afternoon, I was cleaning the deck, when my bucket of water fell over. Well, I presume it fell over, mind you, someone might have knocked it over. By the end of the day, I had solved the water problem with my trusty mop and was beginning to get somewhere.

After a couple of days, I started to get the hang of it. Lenny had gone on leave for a few days, and it was more peaceful without his loud screaming voice around the place. That afternoon, Andy, the steward, and the officers' pantry boy left the ship, and after the arrival of the new steward and pantry boy we sailed for Portland in Dorset.

After about an hour at sea, I suffered my first attack of

seasickness, which I must say is one of the worst things that has ever happened to me. I felt like vomiting but couldn't and there is no place on the ship where you can go to hide from it. The only solution is to face the crisis, which is to stand out on deck and get as much fresh air as possible.

Later that evening, the ship docked at Portland, and was I glad! It had been the roughest sea I could ever have imagined! But to the experienced seaman, it was just calm – as it always is to them. That evening, I just had to get ashore to feel some land beneath my feet. It made me feel a lot better. We were to stay in Portland for another ten days. Then we would start on our long and adventurous voyage.

That weekend, a number of the lads went home on leave, including Dick and the chief cook, Bill, which meant I would have to do Dick's job, and with the chief cook going home that also meant that Lenny would be back. And there I was, assistant to the one and only Lenny, who was quite a laugh really, but could be very mean if you got on the wrong side of him. I made sure I didn't get in his way.

That night, White, the second steward, arranged a party on board, and had asked a number of girls from a nearby holiday camp to come along. So that afternoon, Lenny and myself, who tried to assist, made lots of sandwiches and cakes and other goodies which are needed at parties, while a few of the other lads, were busy stocking up the bar with booze. The tables in the crew mess were removed so that there would be enough room to dance.

That evening, everything started to go just fine – even the captain came down to join in the fun. The girls arrived, about fifteen in all, and a couple of the lads got a bit out of hand, acting like they had never seen a female before.

The bar, being the main attraction, was soon packed. They mustn't have fed those girls back at the holiday camp, for as soon as they saw the sandwiches and cakes, they started to dig in. I felt sorry for one girl there; she had a sandwich in her mouth and was holding a cake in one hand and a drink in the other and one of the lads was dragging her into his cabin, obviously not for a chat.

I left the bar and went into the mess, where all the dancing was going on. As I entered the mess, I was quickly grabbed by a girl, who called herself Honey. Honey was a very well-built girl and was head and shoulders taller than me. She thought I was her teddy bear and found me very cute. I tried to tell her that I wasn't her teddy bear, but it was no good. She just wouldn't let go of me. Anyway, after she had hugged me, and thrown me about the place, Honey eventually crashed out on the deck, and it took several of us to carry her out; we put her in an empty cabin where she could sleep it off.

I went back into the mess and noticed a girl sitting on her own and she was quite a nice-looking girl. I went over to her and asked her to dance.

'I'm afraid I'm not very good at dancing,' she said.

So I sat down next to her and started to talk.

Her name was Carol. She was nineteen and obviously very shy. She didn't drink like the rest of the girls did, just the occasional orange juice. I eventually got her on her feet and we started to dance. I told her that she danced very well.

'That's just because I haven't stood on your feet,' she said.

Well, she did not stand on my feet, but I stood on hers!

By now it was getting late, and one by one, each girl started to disappear into one of the lad's cabins. Now the bar and mess were empty. Carol was now looking at me, more or less saying, well come on then. Aren't you going to take me to see your cabin? I didn't really want to as she looked so innocent and quiet, but they say the quiet ones are the worst! I did really want to say no but being the beast I really am, I quickly took her by the hand and led her to my cabin.

Inside, I played some soft and romantic music. I don't know why; I'm not in the least bit romantic. Anyway, I let it play, and started to kiss Carol who was now no longer the innocent girl I had picked up earlier in the mess, but a right little raver. Her hands were everywhere, mainly trying to undo my trousers; while there I was, trying to help her and help myself at the same time.

Eventually we were both down to our last garments and to the tune of 'O, when the saints go marching in', both of us fell to the floor in hysterics. This was more my tune. I quickly removed Carol's bra and panties. She stayed seated while I put out the light and switched the cassette off. We both ended up in Dick's bunk, which was more suitable as it was on the bottom.

Luckily, breakfast for the crew wasn't until ten o'clock, so I could have a lie-in. We both cuddled up to each other and eventually dropped off.

My bladder must have awakened me early the following morning, so I quickly put my underpants on and rushed out to the toilet to relieve myself. When I returned Carol was just coming to. She asked for the time.

'Just gone eight,' I said.

'As late as that?' she said. She leapt from the bed and started to dress. While she was dressing, she asked if she could come on board that night again to see me. Well, after the night I had just had I couldn't really refuse!

I walked with her to the gangway, where several other girls were waiting. I kissed her goodbye.

'Until tonight, then?' she said. I then ran back through the ship to start cleaning up the mess and help Lenny with the breakfast. By the end of a hard day getting the mess room back to its normal state, I just had enough time to clean the cabin up a bit and have a quick shower before Carol turned up. Just before she arrived, Dick got back from his weekend leave and as we shared the same cabin,

Carol wouldn't be able to stay. Finally she arrived, so I took her along to the bar, where I introduced her to Dick. I had already told him about Carol, and he didn't mind her sleeping in his bed. He had an idea.

'Why don't you tell her to stay and I'll sleep in another cabin until she's asleep, and then I'll creep back and I can have her?'

It seemed okay to me. 'But what if Carol wakes up?' I said.

'Well,' said Dick, 'she won't see who it is in the dark, will she? She'll think it's you next to her.'

Well, Carol stayed that night, and later, in bed, I was thinking about Dick and his idea, and what would happen if Carol woke up and found it wasn't me next to her, but Dirty Dick. Well anyway eventually she fell asleep and I got out of the bed and fetched Dick, who was raring to go. We both crept back into the cabin and I very quietly jumped on the top bunk, while Dick jumped in beside Carol. What if she wakes up? I thought, but I quickly closed my eyes tight and put my hands over my ears, so I couldn't hear a sound, while below me Dick was trying to get Carol on her back. And that's when it happened.

'No, Kev, you've had it for one night. Aren't you ever satisfied?' she said, thinking it was me beside her. Then came the scream, 'You're not Kevin, where's Kevin?'

'Well, it's my bloody bed,' said Dick.

She quickly jumped out, taking a sheet with her, and ran out of the cabin. I put the light on and saw Dick lying naked on his bed.

'What happened then, Dick?' I just couldn't stop laughing. I knew Carol wouldn't be back, so I collected her clothes together and put them outside the cabin. 'Oh well, Dick at least you tried.' Then I got back on my bunk and put the light out.

Chapter Three

The next day flew by, with all the crew back from their leave, and the ship's stores arriving in loads. We were to leave for Gibraltar the following day. It was very hectic, and in the evening most of us went up the road for our last drink in an English pub. I phoned my parents, just to say goodbye and tell them where I was going and when I'd be back. I told them of my first encounter with seasickness. Then I said goodbye and went back to the pub, the Vicky Lodge.

One of the barmen looked just like a woman and a couple of the lads, who by now were out of their minds with booze, were leaning over the counter, trying to pull up his apron to see what colour panties he was wearing. They must have mistaken the apron for a skirt, for he was wearing trousers. Happily enough, he just took it as a laugh, for they didn't mean any harm.

When it came to closing time, we all said goodbye and made our way back to the ship, helping some of those who were unable to help themselves. We sailed the following morning with the HMS *Falmouth*. A small crowd gathered along the quay to see us off, but I didn't pay much attention as I was too busy thinking about seasickness.

We were soon on our way to Gibraltar, a trip which would take us four days. Everyone went about his work except me. I was standing on the poop deck watching England slowly fading away. Just before we sailed the purser, Mr Davies, was taken ill, so they had to replace him.

The new purser's name was Mike Bartley. He joined me on the poop deck to catch a last glimpse of the motherland.

'First trip for you, isn't it, Kevin?'

'Yes, chief,' I replied.

'Oh, well, take a last look. You won't see it for a while.' He then asked about my job and how I was getting on.

I told him it couldn't be better and went inside to clean up for lunch.

*

Usually at sea, when you have finished your duty, the only entertainment is the bar and reading. Most of the lads usually read girlie magazines and just sat back and waited for the next port of call. The four day trip down to Gibraltar soon went by, and like everyone else, I was on deck, just gazing at the Rock, as this was my first foreign port and my first time abroad.

I was excited and eager to get down that gangway so that I could see it for myself. Everyone on board went ashore that night except the odd watchkeepers. I went ashore with two deckhands, John Clayton and Billy Wills who were both familiar with Gibraltar and knew all the best places to go. It was a night of pub-crawling and discos; and rolling back in time to start work again.

The next day, I was given the afternoon off to play football for the ship's team. We were to play another RFA ship called the *Olna* which was berthed behind us. Both teams met as we all boarded the bus to take us to the playing fields, or I should say ash tracks. The weather was hot, and just a bit too hot to play football.

Our team consisted of Dick in goal, the two cooks and a deckhand playing defence, Steve, the deckboy, and three officers playing midfield, and Chippy the carpenter, Jimmy the radio officer and myself attacked. The opposition looked just as rugged. Chippy, who was captain of the side, put me as centre forward. The whistle went and I kicked off, and soon we were running rings round them. Chippy, who was a man in his mid-forties played just like George Best. After about fifteen minutes, with the ball mainly in our possession, Chippy hit a hard shot at the goal, but the goalkeeper couldn't hold it. The ball came to me and I kicked it hard into the back of the net to give us a one goal lead. But it was not for very long. They soon came back and equalised, and even Lenny in defence, who looked ridiculous in his shorts, couldn't stop them.

At half-time we were all close to exhaustion, and the heat didn't help, but we had good support and started the second half looking far the fitter side. We were out there playing for twenty-five minutes and still the scoreline was level. Soon Chippy changed that. He made a move down the left wing and passed the ball to me; all I had to beat was a defender and the goalkeeper. I could see Jimmy on the right wing calling for the ball, so I passed it to him and he hit it hard, straight past the goalkeeper and into the back of the net.

We now looked certain winners, but the Olna men still weren't finished, and, sure enough, they put two goals past Dick to give them the victory they deserved. After the match, good sportsmen that we were, we treated the winners to beers. Also that afternoon, I made sure I didn't forget my family and friends, and I wrote out a few post-cards, letting them know I was fine and having a great time.

We left Gibraltar the next day and were to be at sea for three weeks. Our next port of call was Capetown in South Africa. We had a number of feature films on board, which were to be shown every other night. That broke the boredom a bit. We also picked up a new crew mate before we left Gibraltar. His name was Peter Prowse. He was the new second steward. White, the last second steward had been sacked and flown home.

Chippy had a marvellous scheme going every week. It was eyes down and legs eleven bingo, which we all enjoyed. So we had different things to look forward to. We were also exercising with the Royal Navy. We all found this boring. Every night we had to fasten down the portholes. We were forever refuelling their ships, but eventually I got used to it.

The days were now flying by and seasickness to me was now kid's stuff. Usually when a ship crosses the line (equator) the crew holds a ceremony for the seamen who have never crossed the line before. But, alas, there was no fun on the *Green Rover* that day.

After nearly completing our three weeks at sea, which had been calm ever since we left Gibraltar, we soon felt the Cape beneath us. The ocean became a monster which looked ready for the kill. This was known as the Cape Rollers. It happens where the Atlantic Ocean meets the Indian Ocean – that caused the so-called Rollers. It was fascinating to see, but one had to stay inside the ship, as the waves became so high. It's like the game, 'now you see it, now you don't'. One minute you can see the sky, and the next minute all you can see is the mighty ocean.

That night was terrifying. I had to tie myself in my bunk, as the ship was getting thrown about so much. My cabin was near the officer's pantry and I could hear the smashes and crashes. I hardly slept that night; but when I did turn up for work the next day, everything was in ruins! At least the ship had survived the storm, and we could clean up the place before arriving in Capetown. The crew mess room was in a shambles when I went down; even the huge fridge in the corner of the mess, which had been fastened to the bulkhead, had crashed to the deck.

Chapter Four

After hours of cleaning up, the ship was now looking fairly good, except for a broken fridge and many other things. Table Mountain was now in sight. It felt good to see land again, especially after our little disaster the previous night. The purser went about the ship to see how much South African currency we would need for our week's stay. I asked for forty rand, which was about twenty pounds. We docked that morning, along with several other ships. Our ship was alongside the *Stromness*, a store ship with British officers, but a Chinese crew.

The first time I went ashore, I was carrying a gashbag which normally I just threw over the side, but as we were in port I couldn't. So I went across on to the *Stromness* and down their gangway. There were several big bins on the quay and each was watched by a black man. I didn't even hesitate, but threw the gashbag in the first bin I came to. As soon as I threw the bag in, the man watching it quickly jumped in, but I knew he would not find anything.

That evening, we all went ashore. At the end of the quay were a number of taxis. Each taxi had 'No blacks' painted on its side. I'm not colour-prejudiced in the least, as there were a couple of black guys on our ship. We used to have a laugh with them, and they just took it in fun. Because of their colour, they couldn't ride in the taxis, so they had to walk. Most of us walked with them in disgust.

We ended up in a nightclub called The Navigator's Den, which had plenty of girls and a black group playing a lot of soul music which was great. But the club didn't allow black people in, which I thought was bad. They literally treat them like dirt! But we ignored their rules and did as we pleased.

I went ashore the following night to see a movie. When I got inside, I lit a cigarette, as I thought one could smoke. But I was immediately told to put it out. So I left the cinema in anger. Anyway, the film was a load of rubbish, so I walked up the street to the first bar I came to. Little did I know at the time that it was for blacks only, but I stayed and had a few drinks and no one seemed to mind.

I then tried to signal a taxi but none would stop. I walked along the street a bit. There were many cars parked alone the roadside. In between two cars was a scooter. I wasn't then and never will be a thief. I just made use of this scooter and had a little go. (Well, there was no one about at the time.) I started the scooter and rode down the main street, and, after having a bit of fun, I parked the scooter in a back alley, quite near The Navigator's Den, but then decided not to go in. I signalled a taxi ready to go back to the ship. The taxi driver was black which I found a bit odd when on the side of his car was painted 'No blacks'.

I asked him if he knew of a place with girls.

'You want a girl?' he said, 'I'll get you a girl.'

I must have cheered him up, for when I had got in he looked as miserable as sin. He drove around a couple of blocks and finally stopped outside a restaurant. He said he wouldn't be long and went inside. About five minutes later he came out accompanied by a girl. She looked quite nice, and she sat next to me in the back. She quickly put her hand down my trousers and before I knew where I was, she was hard at work on my neck.

The taxi driver drove like a mad man, up into the mountains to an area we had been told to stay away from. We stopped miles from anywhere. The taxi driver got out, saying he would be back in half an hour.

The girl – I didn't quite catch her name, started to undress. 'I'll give you a good time,' she said, but before we started to do anything, she got out of the taxi to do a pee.

This turned me off right away. She was soon back in the car, and attacked me with her big boobs dangling in front of my face.

After what she had called a good time, the taxi driver came back to the car. As we straightened ourselves up, the taxi driver made his way back to town. I knew that the taxi bill would be quite high and that the girl wasn't offering her services for nothing, but all I had on me was six rand. The taxi driver asked where abouts in town I wanted to go. I told him to go to The Navigator's Den, which was the only place I really know.

After about fifteen minutes, the taxi arrived at a place which looked familiar, but I wasn't certain. He then gave me his bill, which was fifteen rand for the taxi and twenty-five rand for the young lady's services. With six rand in my pocket, I didn't know what to do. I told them that I didn't quite have that amount on me.

I was wearing a black leather jacket which was quite expensive. So I offered him my jacket and wrist watch plus the six rand. He hummed and hawed and not being much of a business man he didn't know where to turn. The girl sat there, saying nothing. The taxi driver got out of the car and opened my door. I also got out and started to take off my jacket.

The driver was now busy talking to the girl and I had my jacket half on and half off, as I didn't really want to part with it. I put it on and buttoned it up, and took one more look at the taxi driver, who was still leaning through the car window talking to the girl. Sod it, I thought, now is my chance, and I ran for it with the voice of the taxi driver saying, 'I'll get you!' I ran down an unlit road with the head lights of the taxi shining on my neck. There was a small alley leading off the road.

I was quickly down the alley and on to the main street. Along the street I passed a restaurant which was for whites only, so I went inside, feeling quite safe and secure. I ordered a coffee and a cheese roll and sat down by the window watching out for the taxi.

After peering through the window for nearly half an hour, I left for The Navigator's Den which was just up the street. As I approached The Den, I saw a taxi standing outside. It looked just like the taxi from which I had had my narrow escape. I made sure the driver didn't see me, as I hid in a doorway praying for it to leave.

My prayer was answered when a couple of drunken sailors got into the taxi and left. I went inside and met up with a couple of lads from the ship. I told them all about my adventure with a laugh, but at the time it was no laugh. I arrived back on board at about two in the morning and I made sure I didn't get the same taxi again.

I woke early that Sunday morning, wishing I could stay in bed, but I had to get cracking as I had the afternoon off to play football for the ship's team. We were playing the *Stromness* that afternoon. Both teams boarded a bus which was waiting at the end of the quay. It was quite a long journey on the old bus. Their team consisted of mainly Chinese players, except for a big-headed engineer cadet, who was captain and he couldn't play football. He needn't have bothered playing, as they hammered us eight two and one of our goals was an own goal by their captain. The other came from Steve the deckboy. He scored just before the end of the match.

That evening, I visited the local Seamen's Mission where I wrote out a few postcards and a very long letter to my mother, telling her all was well at my end, and how I was enjoying myself.

As I had a late night the night before, I went back early. I must have turned in about nine-thirty, as I had to be up the next day when we were to leave Capetown for a two week break as they say, until we came to the hectic port of Mombasa in Kenya.

I had a dream that night, but it seemed very real. I dreamt that the taxi driver and the girl caught me and tortured me for the forty rand which I owed them. They took me to an area from which no white man had ever emerged alive. Well, meet the first, as silly as it seems. I escaped my jailers to breathe once more. That's when I woke up to find myself in my bunk on the *Green Rover* as safe as houses. But I wouldn't be for much longer as I'd have the chief cook running after me with a meat cleaver!

I was late getting up, but I felt great. The ship was ready to leave Capetown and I hadn't done a thing. As I cleaned up the breakfast plates, I looked through one of the port-holes for a last look at Capetown wondering whether I'd ever step on those shores again, and thinking of the taxi driver and the girl, knowing how much they'd like to meet up with me again.

I felt a bit sad on leaving Capetown, but was even more excited about Mombasa. The days started to fly by, with bingo and films, and darts matches. Then, during the day, Lenny told us of his previous experiences in Mombasa, which certainly made the going much better.

We were racing at the time, with a frigate called *The Lowestoft*. I was standing out on deck with one of the stewards. He was looking through his binoculars at two distant ships.

'They are Russians,' he said.

I took a look and found he was right. One was a destroyer, the other an aircraft carrier. The race with the frigate was now over. The two Russian ships, which were now miles away, seemed to have been taking notes of what had been going on. I stayed on deck and watched the two distant figures fade away. Then I went inside to get some work done.

I didn't see any more Russian ships after that. Maybe they pretend that they're the fairies who only come out in the open every now and then. That evening was my lucky one, as I won at bingo three times. As Mombasa was now only a day away, everyone went past their limit that night and had one for the girl he would see the next evening. Lenny had about six which didn't mean he was thirsty!

The ship anchored in the harbour the following morning, and Lenny, who was accompanied by Pete, the second steward, was ready for the boat to take them ashore. The only thing wrong with a boat is that you can only get ashore every half hour and not when you like, as I found out later when I was ready to go ashore with a few of the lads.

I got to the ladder which you had to climb down to get into the boat. I put my foot on the first rung and then felt the breeze – I had split my trousers. I ran quickly to my cabin to change, but when I returned the boat had gone. So I had to wait for the next boat. The half hour soon went by and before long the boat was back at the ship.

I climbed down the ladder and jumped rearing to go. Pang, the little Chinese laundryman, got in the boat with me, and as he had visited Mombasa before, I asked if I could go along with him. He seemed pleased at this as he was on his own. The boat reached the shore and we got into a waiting taxi.

Pang told the driver where to go in town. We drove along the street, which was packed with stalls mainly selling wooden carvings. We passed under two great elephant tusks, which stretched right across the street. We were now in the busy part of Mombasa. The taxi stopped outside a bar and Pang, who insisted on paying the fare, paid the driver, making sure he wasn't overcharged.

We then went inside, where we were greeted by at least a dozen girls. After trying to get free, we made our way to the bar and, still with a few hangers-on, we managed to get a drink for ourselves and sat down. The bar was empty except for Pang and myself and a dozen screaming jungle bunnies.

Pang told me to take my time and not rush into anything, but I was raring to go. A few girls sat around our table, asking for drinks, and one girl there stuck to me like glue. She sat right on my lap – where it hurts, to be precise.

'Come on, John,' she said. 'How about a good time?'

Well, I was in no situation to refuse. She just looked liked the rest, so I didn't grumble.

I knocked back my beer, and went upstairs, leaving Pang surrounded by all those girls. I was now entering my first brothel and I was looking forward to it very much. As it was very hot, we didn't need any sheets. Then came the crunch. I had to pay her before anything could happen – one hundred shillings, which was five pounds! Well, as I had never visited a place quite like this before I gave her the money. She put it in a hole in the middle of her mattress. She then undid her dress, and so I used my common sense and started to take off my clothes too and as she was undressed before I was, she helped me with my trousers and underpants.

It was very dark in the room and I couldn't make out her body. All I could see was a dark figure, which spoke very broken English. She sat me down on the bed and started to laugh. She called me a cherry boy, which means nothing else but a virgin. Well, I soon showed her my cherry and she was soon working for the money I had just paid her.

She called herself Florence and, with a laugh, I said, 'You're more like Dougal.' But obviously she had never seen the *Magic Roundabout*.

She got up to get a drink of water, so I asked her if she

would get me one as well. She slipped into her dress and left the room. I didn't really like paying for anything, especially for a woman. So I felt for the hundred shillings in the mattress and started to dress. With my shoes in one hand and grasping the money in the other, I made a quick exit from the room. I went into a nearby toilet to put my shoes on. I then opened the door to see if all was clear, but Florence was outside talking to another girl. I waited for a minute until she had passed. Then I went outside and ran down the stairs.

Pang was no longer in the bar; his patience had probably given out and he had gone upstairs with some girl. I ran through the bar, ignoring any girl who approached me, and then ran up the street. I think that is the only thing I am really good at – running! I just hoped I wouldn't bump into Florence any more.

I walked for a good bit, gazing through the shop windows. Then a man approached me and asked if I wanted a white girl. I quickly said I did. I followed him for about five minutes until we came to some rackety old shacks. We went inside one where a number of girls with young children were sitting gossiping like old hens. I was shown into a bedroom, where I was greeted by an Indian girl. I was shocked on not seeing a white girl, although I didn't really mind what colour she was. The man who brought me there was her pimp, and a rough one at that. I could see the marks and bruises on her body where he had beaten her. They talked together outside, leaving me alone in the room. I felt the bed, which was very comfortable. The girl came back into the room and told me how much her fee was, eighty shillings which I agreed to, as Florence had charged me a hundred. I gave her the money and the pimp was soon taking his share, which was well over two thirds. He then left.

The girl had a typical Indian name, Jasmine. She also

had a baby girl and she was fond of cats, and had several roaming around. The girl who lived next door was free for that night, so she looked after Jasmine's daughter while we set about our business, which I thought was very enjoyable. To Jasmine, who must have been at least twenty-four and used to her profession, I must have been just the same as anyone else. It's a pity that a girl like Jasmine had to do such work to support her daughter and herself.

She told me that she enjoyed her work and had been a prostitute for nearly ten years. Her father had put her up to it as they were poor, and needed the money. She had long, jet-black hair and was very attractive. Her body was that of a model and she had the eyes of a tiger. As I didn't have to be back on board ship the following day, I just stayed in bed with Jasmine, whom I held close to my body. She spoke quite good English, not like Florence, who, compared to Jasmine, was just a wench.

I told her whereabouts in England I came from and what it was like there. Jasmine had longed to travel, but had never left Kenya. Her parents had come to live in Mombasa thirty years before. They arrived by boat from India, and Jasmine was born in Mombasa and had lived there ever since.

The next day, as I left, she asked if I would come back to see her. I said I would. She was like a doll standing there. I felt like putting her in my pocket and taking her home with me, but I left, knowing I probably wouldn't see her again.

I waved down a taxi to take me back to the ship but I didn't quite feel up to the ship at that time, so I asked the driver to take me to a place called Sunshine Bar, which I had heard Lenny speak of. The taxi cost me five shillings. I paid him and went inside; it was dark. I walked towards the bar and ordered a drink.

A woman, the size of an elephant, approached me. She was the mamma in the bar and was in charge of all the girls.

She asked me if I wanted a girl. I thought it was a bit early for one but with a bit of persuasion from the mamma, I was quickly choosing, as I didn't really want to argue. She was a lot bigger than me.

There were quite a number of girls sitting down at the tables. I had a good look and finally walked over to a small girl sitting alone. I said 'Hello!' and sat down. It was a bit early in the day for drinking and the place was empty. The girl got very chatty, asking what ship I was on, and what I did. After about an hour, the bar started to fill up with sailors. By that time in the day, most of the girls had got their hands full. One girl was at the bar pulling at a sailor's arm to take her home.

Then Lenny and Pete appeared in the doorway. Both were out of their minds from booze. They weren't on their own for long; both were swept of their feet by a number of girls. The girl whom I was with was called Suzanne. I asked if she had a nice place.

'It's okay,' she said. 'Why? Do you want to go there now?'

By this time I was ready for Suzanne, so I grabbed her by the hand and left by the back way. Suzanne must have been only about four foot eleven and very fragile, so I had to be careful, making sure I didn't break her.

I kept on asking, if we were nearly there, but all I got was, 'Yes, it's just around the corner.' She lived in a flat, and by the look of the place from the outside, I didn't expect any miracles. We went inside and climbed the stone steps to her room.

It was quite cosy, although there was nowhere to sit down. Her huge double bed took up most of the room, so I lay on her bed, which was very bouncy. While I was busy bouncing up and down on her bed, she was feeding her cat, which had a small basket in the corner of the room. She asked me if I wanted anything to eat and I was glad she asked me, I was really hungry not having eaten since the night before.

I felt like nicking the cat's grub.

'What's cooking then?' I asked.

'Steak.'

'Steak, yeah, my favourite.' They often ate steak out there; it couldn't have been very dear if they ate it that often. Later I found out that it was just horse meat and it was like chewing leather, but the gravy was all right.

After the toughest steak I had ever eaten, I asked her where the toilet was. I was shown next door, and all it was was a hole in the ground. No way was I going to use that, I'd have done myself an injury. I just had to hold myself until I could find a decent place.

In Suzanne's room, being so small both of us had to be comfortable just with a bed. She wore her panties, as it was hot. She had a small fan on the ceiling which didn't work and it was no good opening a window. We lay there side by side, with the sweat pouring from our bodies. She started to drop off but I had a better idea and kept her moving all night.

Her room was really quite bare; just her bed, a small wardrobe and drawers, also the cat and his basket. I only stayed until about ten that evening, as I had to return to work the next day. I was all ready and waiting for Suzanne who was sprucing herself up; getting ready for the next lad who would take her home, chew the leather steak and shit in the stone hole.

After hurrying her with her dress, we made our way down the stairs, where a taxi was conveniently waiting. She told him that she wanted to go to the Sunshine Bar and that I wanted to go back to the ship. By this time Suzanne hadn't asked for any money. I thought my luck was in. The taxi arrived at the Sunshine Bar and Suzanne asked me for some money to get a drink. I gave her twenty shillings but she said the drink she wanted cost forty shillings. Without arguing, I gave her the money as it wasn't much and I said goodbye to Suzanne. Then the taxi drove off for the ship.

This time the taxi fare came to ten shillings. I only had five on me. I asked if five would be enough. But he insisted on ten. Mike Bartley was also arriving back in a taxi and I asked him if he would be kind enough to lend me the five shillings to satisfy the angry driver. We both waited for the boat to take us out to the ship and as we waited we spoke of our escapades around the town. He asked if I had enjoyed myself in the brothels. Of course, I didn't tell him right down to the actual details. The boat soon came and took us out to the ship. I invited Mike down to our bar for a drink. I just had a beer but he had a double whisky on the rocks. The bar was empty except for the quartermaster of the watch and old Ted the signalman who was well drunk.

We sat there, drinking until the early hours of the morning. He asked if my job was okay. I said it was just fine. Then he mentioned going up top to work in the officer's pantry, as Pete the second steward didn't get on well with the pantry boy, a John Scotchford, who was very cheeky. They all called him Val for short, as his middle name was Valentine. Little did I know that day that he had gotten into a fight with Dick. Straight away I took a disliking to Val whom I rarely ever spoke to out of choice. I had a grudge against him, as Dick who was a good friend to me, had been beaten up by him that day.

Chapter Five

It was late when I turned in and Dick was fast asleep in his bunk. He could lie in the following morning, as he had done my job while I was ashore gallivanting around the brothels and having a good time. It was nice to be back sleeping in my own bunk again, but I was greedy; just sex-mad really, wishing that one of those girls I had had could be with me now.

I only slept for two hours, when I was awakened by the drunken quarter-master, who had spent most of his time in the bar. I washed and dressed, leaving the cabin and Dick, the sleeping beauty, looking so peaceful lying there, with his eyes closed and mouth wide open.

The next morning I went to work in the mess and helped Bill prepare the breakfast. During the day we weren't short of help, for a number of native boys were on board doing various jobs. One of the boys helped me in the mess room and the galley as Dick was away. The boy had the right old proper name of Charles. I called him Charlie, and Charlie worked for just a few shillings a day, which Dick and I paid for.

There weren't many to feed at breakfast, as on most days we had either bacon or sausages, and as the boys were mainly Muslims, they would not eat pork. Dinner was a completely different matter. It was like feeding the hungry thousands. After a busy day, I washed and changed, went ashore and went to the Sunshine Bar. I was immediately grabbed by the balls. The girls do this instead of shaking hands. The girl who had chosen to grab me was huge and had a deep voice. She said, 'You want a nice clean girl, boy?'

She pointed over to a girl who looked very innocent, but I thought was probably just as well practised as her sisters.

I didn't argue, as her big sister was now hurting me. She let go and hit me on the back, laughing as she said, 'Now you take care of my little sister, you hear!'

Not even having a drink, I left the premises with this timid-looking cat, and went to a place I was not quite used to. It was an apartment right next door to the Sunshine Bar. It was very clean with a shower and bath and a proper bog.

Great, I thought. I looked at the girl who still looked very timid.

Maybe she's a virgin. Then I thought of the price. I asked her and she whispered her first words.

'Forty shillings.'

'What?' I said.

'Oh is that too much?' she replied.

'No, it's just right,' I said.

We took a shower together. The girl's name was Sarah, and she was very skinny, but for a girl of her size, she had tremendous boobs. I dried her and laid her on the nice clean sheets. It was like a palace, fit for a king and queen. I lay beside her and started to kiss her. Sarah was a very small girl, and I don't mean in height – and I did feel it. I screamed blue murder. There was blood everywhere. I dashed to the bathroom for some toilet paper. The poor girl was on the bed in agony and so was I. I had just split my bloody foreskin! And did it bleed! After lapping the room a dozen times, holding it with toilet paper, the bleeding stopped. Sarah looked okay lying down, but when she walked to the bathroom she looked as if she were going to lay an egg.

I dressed in agony. I offered Sarah the forty shillings, but she wouldn't accept it, as we had not enjoyed ourselves. I left and jumped into a taxi which took me to HMS *Blake*. I went on board to see the doctor. He had a look, along with a few spectators.

'Nasty!' they said. He gave it a proper wash, and had another inspection. He put some cream on it and gave me some tablets to take. 'It's not so bad, now,' he said, 'and another thing before you go – lay off the girls for a bit.'

I took his advice and went back to the ship. I was in tears as it hurt so much. It was about nine o'clock when I got back on board and I went straight to my cabin to see if it had started to bleed again. It wasn't bleeding, but it looked a right mess. I took one of the tablets and went straight to bed. I had a painful night, lying on my back with the sheets away from my body.

I woke early that morning and took another tablet. I grabbed a towel and made for the shower. Inside, I took a look at what I thought was a sight for sore eyes, but after washing it, it didn't look bad at all. I felt much better now and went back to the cabin and dressed. I woke Dick up and told him what had happened. He laughed with a yawn and went back to sleep.

I was washing the tablets down, when Geoff, the radio officer, who organised the football teams came in. He had arranged a match with a college team ashore and asked if I would play. The match was scheduled for Sunday, and we only had a small crew, so there were not many to choose from. I took a look at his sheet of paper, which didn't hold many names, except himself, Jimmy, the other radio officer, and Chippy. 'You can count on me,' I said. Then he went through to the galley to see Bill and Dick, who both volunteered.

Most of the lads went ashore that night, and as I didn't want to be the odd man out, I went along as well. I got into a taxi with three donkey greasers, Tony Barrett, Fred Tindall and old Taff, who was no stranger to those parts.

We went to a small night club called The Buccaneer. All three men had girls waiting for them, and old Taff's girl must have been the youngest. All night I danced with a girl who was great fun to be with, but as the hours got nearer to closing, I started to worry. I knew she would want me to go back to her place and I wanted to – but I thought of the doctor's advice.

Believe it or not, old Taff, who must have been at least sixty-five was the first one out of the door with his little sparrow under his arm! The girl who clung so tight to me was called Kala.

'Come,' she said, 'we go and do it now eh?'

I was trying to delay her for as long as possible and ordered another drink.

Tony and Fred said, 'What are you waiting for? Go with her.' Then they both left.

By now Kala was getting very impatient. I was trying to calm her down by telling her I didn't feel very well and that I would see her the following night when I might be feeling a little bit better. I eventually got to the doorway, with Kala hanging on to my arm. She was now screaming, 'Don't go, I want you.'

'No,' I said, 'not tonight, I'll see you tomorrow.'

She finally let go of my arm and I went out into the dark street and got into a taxi.

After breakfast the following day, we started to prepare the cold buffet. Lenny and Pete were back on board giving a helping hand, as they were to play for the team that afternoon. The match was to start at two o'clock. Finally all was finished in the galley and the buffet was on show in the mess. We all changed into our kit and assembled on deck, where Geoff called out our names to see if all were present; all were, so, we climbed down the ladder into the boat which took us ashore.

A bus was waiting to take us to the college, a ten minute

journey. Passing through the markets in the streets, the day was very hot and humid. We arrived, all eager to get out on to the field to show off our talents, with Dick in goal, trying to look the part of the England goalkeeper.

Our opponents received a huge cheer as they came out on to the field in their green and yellow strip. The match soon got underway, the college kicking off. They soon showed their skills, as they were young, fast and very fit, and were soon running rings around us. In fact they were so good, you would have thought they were professionals. They started to knock in the goals, and not even Dick, who stood between them and the goal, could stop them. Every time I received the ball, I had a defender taking it away from me and clearing it way up the field. Not once did we get a chance to score, in fact I lost count of how many goals they knocked in. After the cat and mouse game, our side looked knackered, and the score must have been at least twenty–nil.

Orange juice was supplied after the game, so I took a glass of this magic potion and lay on the grass. The college team said they had enjoyed the match and left for the changing rooms. After a while we felt our old selves. We climbed on the bus and went back to the ship, but I don't think any one who played football that day went ashore. I couldn't imagine anyone having the strength to face up to a female; well, not that night anyway.

The following evening, everyone went ashore, as it was our last night in Mombasa. There was plenty of beer swallowed that night. The ship sailed for Karachi the following day, and I stood on deck watching the golden sands of Kenya slowly going out of sight. That evening I wrote home to my parents whom I would not see for another seven months. At that moment, feeling very homesick, I finished off the letter and turned in.

★

The following week was very hot the sea was calm and nearly every day a school of dolphins swam along beside the ship, accompanied by a number of flying fish. The dolphins jumped out of the water and plunged back in, just as if they were putting on their own circus show for us.

Our stay in Karachi was very short. I went ashore just once to get some Christmas cards to send home. It was a very dirty place, with rats running wild in the streets. Eventually, myself and my companion, Billy Witts, lost ourselves and it was no good asking anyone for no one spoke English. Then Billy noticed a stand of carts drawn by cows with a small boy at the front of each cart. I approached the first cart and asked the boy if he could take us to the ship.

'Okay,' he said, 'that will be ten rupees.'

So we both climbed upon the smelly cart and set off.

The boy used the whip on the old cow pulling the cart, but it still didn't go any faster. I could have walked faster than that cow. After about twenty minutes there wasn't a ship in sight. We were both getting very bad tempered and told the boy again that we wanted to go to the ship. Finally we came to a halt, the boy saying that his cow was very tired and he thought it would pack up and die if he didn't get home.

We both gave up hope and jumped down from the cart, not knowing what direction to take. The boy said good-night and shot off at full gallop – that cow could have won the Derby at the speed he was going!

We both fell to the ground with laughter. Billy said if she was on a motorway back home, the law would have her for speeding. We eventually found our way back to the ship.

We left Karachi the following day for the Persian Gulf. We made two stops up the Gulf, one at Bahrain, where we refuelled on a jetty, which was a bit longer than the pier at Southend-on-Sea! Our second stop was at Banda Abbas in Iran. It was just a social call. We went ashore, but personally I didn't like the place and was glad to leave, what with seeing all those Arabs driving across dirt tracks in big Rolls Royce cars, and the fact that the bars never had any beer and the barmaids found great enjoyment in picking their noses and chewing the result – very appetising!

We left the famous Persian Gulf, which is very well known for its oil, wealth, hot weather and many sharks. I suppose to the sharks it's the French Riviera. I wouldn't fancy swimming there, but the captain told us on leaving the Gulf, 'I know it was hot and not very exciting, but you must go there to pass through the famous Arabian "Hole in the wall", which is a narrow passage, just big enough for a ship of our size to pass through.'

★

After spending nearly six weeks crossing the Indian ocean, we finally made it to Singapore. To most of the seamen who had visited Singapore before it was nothing special, but to me it was heaven. The day we arrived the sun was shining, and it was just before Christmas. We had every kind of salesman on board, trying to sell us a lot of old rubbish.

They say the first night ashore is the best – well it wasn't for me. The local village was called Somberwang. It had its bars, brothels and shops; you name it and Somberwang had it. That first night, everyone piled into the bars, and you couldn't really blame us for we had been at sea for six weeks.

The brothel, the one in the village, was situated behind the bars. So, accompanied by many others I made tracks for the glowing red lights. It reminded me of being at a cattle auction where you pick the one of your choice. Eventually my turn came, and as there wasn't much on the shelf left to pick from, I finally chose a little Chinese woman who must have been old enough to be my mother – and she was a black belt in karate.

I paid for the time with the woman, which was more like a Karate lesson, than sex. I then went into one of the bars, where I found a couple of the lads drunk. I think you have to be drunk to stay out of trouble as I soon found out.

As I entered another bar, someone on the inside was coming out. They were swing-doors. I got to the door first, and as I couldn't see through the frosted glass, it swung right into the oncomer's face. I said I was sorry, but that wasn't enough, and I soon felt his large fist. He must have been six feet four inches tall, and almost as wide. He was a New Zealand soldier based in the Nee Soon. His size made me run. I ran straight into the next bar, which was almost empty; but Tony Barrett and John Clayton were there. They were both sitting on stools at the bar and both were drunk. I told them about the bloke who hit me and no sooner had I said that, than I was struck again. I hit the floor like a brick. Barrett and Clayton were soon up on their feet, but there were too many for them to handle.

There must have been about eight of them, and Barrett and Clayton, who were both drunk, didn't last long. I tried to get up, but was soon knocked down. I thought I was going to die, as they kicked me so many times. I noticed Barrett lying opposite me; he was covered in blood, and I was the cause of it all. I too, was in a bad way. All I remember is someone in a uniform helping me to my feet. Clayton didn't look so bad, but they carried Barrett out on a stretcher. The bar looked like something out of a Western, with broken bottles and chairs all over the place.

When I got outside, the street was packed with people; we were certainly in the limelight. The military police took the soldiers away, while we were taken to the hospital. John Clayton just had a few bruises, but they kept Barrett in hospital for a couple of days, as he had suffered a broken nose and jaw; and another lad called Gillespie, who was coming into the bar at the same time as the soldiers, had suffered a serious stab wound.

They kept me in until the following day. I had been knocked unconscious and received many cuts and bruises to the head and body. I gave the military police a statement that night, and the following morning they gave me some clothes to wear, as mine had been ripped off me. Then they took me back to the ship.

I was still dazed when I returned to the ship. What a day – it was Christmas Eve, I didn't do any work that day – I just slept. But that evening I went to a small party, felt fine and had a good time.

The next morning was all work and no play. We all worked very hard for breakfast and lunch, but the evening meal was cancelled and a cold buffet was put on in its place, so that all the catering staff could have the afternoon off, as it was Christmas Day.

I went into Singapore City that afternoon with a few of the lads, and had a smashing time up Bugis Street in the heart of town. We looked through Lions City and had a meal at Fatty's, the well-known eating place in China Town. Bugis Street is well known for its transvestites, and believe you me, you can't tell the difference.

The following day, Tony Barrett was back on board with a face full of plaster. He was accompanied by a New Zealand army sergeant, all ready with more questions for Barrett and myself. We went in to see him individually and after many questions he told us we might still be needed. He then left it at that. That evening there was no shore leave for the catering staff, as the captain was giving a huge cocktail party which was held on the flight deck. It was set for three hundred guests, but more like six hundred eventually turned up. Among them were lords, ladies, admirals and generals, and all kinds of other people. There was a lot of food eaten that night, and a lot of booze drunk; it was one hell of a do, and there was a lot of cleaning up afterwards.

*

Our stay in Singapore was going quite well, until a rumour went about that we might have to go to Darwin in Northern Australia where there had been a flooding disaster, but finally we were not needed. So we carried on enjoying ourselves. On New Year's Eve, we all made our way to Bugis Street in the heart of Singapore. That night I should have done a Cinderella and been back on board by midnight to ring in the New Year; as I was the youngest crew member, but I didn't know. Dick, who stayed on board that night, did the ringing in of the New Year while old Taff rang out the Old Year. As we were seven and a half hours in front of UK time we were still celebrating the New Year in the crew bar at seven-thirty the following morning.

By now our pockets had holes in them, and as we were spending a month in Hong Kong next trip, most of us were just wondering where our money would come from. I received a silver St Christopher and chain from my mother that day for a Christmas present. So I thought maybe St Christopher would find me some money. I bought myself a Christmas present too – a Japanese Seiko watch. You get things like that for next to nothing. The ship left Singapore on 7th January, 1975, bound for Hong Kong, the place I had always dreamed of going to ever since I saw the film 'Suzie. Wong.' That's the trouble with me – I watch too many films.

*

We travelled through four days of heavy rain. In Hong Kong at that time of year it is winter and the island suffers from a great deal of rainfall. This is known as monsoon weather. Hong Kong was breathtaking to see all the junks in the harbour, and getting the smell of fish, was all very exciting. But after spending nearly three hundred pounds in Singapore, my bank balance on the ship was very low.

We were lucky, for our captain had the gift of the gab and got the ship right alongside in Tamar Barracks, while most of the other ships had to anchor out in the harbour. It wasn't a long walk ashore for us. The China Fleet club was practically next door, and beyond that was Wanchai with its playboy clubs, and what have you.

On the opposite side of the ship were the Star ferry boats which went back and forth to Kowloon. That first night ashore I wanted to do so much. But even though we were all skint, we still went ashore amongst the fast-moving, and hectic traffic of Hong Kong. The first stop was at the China Fleet club which is huge. It has its bars, dining rooms, gaming machines, roulette tables and bingo, where you could win as much as a thousand pounds in one night.

After the bingo had ended we were still no richer, and we made our way to Wanchai, better known as Drug City. The place was one big opium den, with many pushers on street corners. Most of these pushers were also pimps as well. They would tell you the prices of their girls and what the girls would do. But nothing was new to us. We just wanted to look around and find out the best places to go, which varied from the Californian Bar to the Dolphin Bar. Most were really much the same; prices didn't differ – it was still expensive, especially when you bought a girl a drink.

We soon found a small bar, just off the main drag, which

was to become our local. It was the Paradise Bar. It was a small place and a bit cheaper than most of the other bars. The girls in the Paradise weren't the prettiest girls in the city but we made do!

Wanchai never closed. You could drink until you dropped and no one would care; most of us returned to the ship by taxi. There were other means of transportation such as walking or taking a rickshaw. The only trouble with a rickshaw is that it's twice as dear as a taxi and of course very much slower.

As Hong Kong was so expensive you couldn't really go ashore every night. The television was quite exciting. Hong Kong has one TV station, which never closes and always shows feature films during the day. Many salesmen came on board. Many of them were tailors and anything you wanted made, they would do and at quite a reasonable price.

I had a leather jacket, two pairs of trousers and two shirts made and all to measure, for about thirty-five pounds.

There was also a blind man who made lampshades in the form of Chinese houses, and another man, asked for any photograph of your family which he would transfer to a plate, and for less than a pound.

After being in Hong Kong for about a week, I decided to go ashore again, as I had a bit more money. I went ashore with Dick and Steve, the deckboy. We all decided to go across on the Star ferry to Kowloon. We queued with many others mostly office workers, returning home. The price of the crossing was fifty cents, about three English pence; you could go either upstairs or downstairs. As we crossed the harbour, a plane was landing on the runway which juts out into the harbour.

The crossing was quick and soon everyone was gathering at the port side of the ferry to disembark. We made our way up the street, which was much cleaner than that of Wanchai. I noticed a sign on a wall: it was a picture of a Chinese youth with the words 'Wanted for Murder'. Below the picture was a lot of Chinese writing, and below that it said a reward of six thousand dollars was offered (about five hundred pounds). We looked at each other, wondering whether to go on or not. We went on. Kowloon was much cleaner than Wanchai. It had its clubs and sauna baths, and in some ways it resembled Soho in London.

Obviously Kowloon was for the more executive types! We entered a place called the Ritz, which was very elegant, with topless barmaids. You were warned before you entered the premises that you could look but you mustn't touch if you knew what was good for you. Most of the girls were European and Australian. We sat down and watched the go-go dancers performing on stage. Then one of the barmaids came over and asked for our order.

I thought I'd be very extravagant, so I ordered a Harvey Wallbanger which consists of vodka, galliano and orange juice. The girl who served us was Australian, a big blonde girl. She wore black tights and panties, with a small white apron around her waist and she walked gracefully up and down in her tall black stiletto, heeled shoes. She was a very, big-busted girl with very large, protruding nipples. When she returned with our drinks, I felt like complementing her on her fine pair, but I didn't, as I'm too shy!

We had one more drink in the Ritz before leaving, making sure this time that I had a beer – it was cheaper. We had a good look around Kowloon before going into a bar, the Jolly Swagman, which was very old. There was a man at the piano, playing Waltzing Matilda, and there were a few of the lads from the ship inside, downing their pints of ale. We had quite an enjoyable evening before making our way back to the ship.

*

For the next couple of days, I was quite content to stay on board watching television and drinking in the bar. In the mess was a notice about a trip arranged by the Seamen's Mission to take a number of the ship's crew across to Kowloon, through the new territories and then up to the Chinese border. I quickly put my name down for the trip.

I went ashore and up to Victoria to send home some postcards. I walked around all the small back streets seeing all the different things the people were making. It was mostly clothes and toys; nearly all that sort of thing is made in Hong Kong, such as the little novelty toys that go into Christmas crackers. I looked around most of the shops and market places, where the smell of fish was so strong it could knock you down!

I got the afternoon off for the trip to the Chinese border. About twenty of us went in all. We made our way to the ferry with a priest, a Father Banyon from the Seamen's Mission. We crossed the ferry and made our way to the Hong Kong Hilton where many a famous person has stayed. We all boarded a coach and met our guide for the trip, a Chinese girl who spoke perfect English. She told us her name was Nancy.

The coach travelled out of Kowloon and on to the New Territories. We went up and down hills, through small villages, and right around a big lake with lots of fancy houses situated around it. It took us nearly an hour before we reached our destination, which was a huge forest with a small lake below it, and on the lake was a Chinese junk. Nancy told us that the junk was now a museum.

We went on board. It sold all kinds of souvenirs. I bought Chairman Mao's *Little Red Book* – in English of course. There was also a small snack bar where we all had some refreshment before going on. We climbed up a very steep path through the forest until we reached the top, where there was a small park with a number of telescopes and a lookout tower with a guard inside. Beyond that was a huge barbed-wire fence, and beyond that was Communist China. You could see for miles, with the hills in the background.

I looked through one of the telescopes at a long road where I could see a Chinese sentry on guard. I was amazed to think that I was looking at a country which had shut itself off from the world; a country with a vast population, which believed in one god – their own – Chairman Mao! There was an old couple sitting together on a bench, dressed in traditional Chinese clothes, and you could have your picture taken with them for five dollars. I was more interested in looking through the telescope.

We finally left the view of China and the old couple and made our way back to Kowloon. We didn't go straight back to the ship; we went first to the Seamen's Mission with Father Banyon and Nancy. We had an interesting discussion on our problems and experiences and all the fine places we had visited on our voyage.

*

The sun didn't shine at all during our stay in Hong Kong, but we enjoyed ourselves all the same. Our stay was for almost a month, but it soon came to an end. The night before we left we had one more night in Wanchai at the Paradise Bar. Most of the lads were woman-hunting that night and so was I! Dick and myself went to a small apartment high above Wanchai which someone had told us about.

I think it was the second floor from the top. We went up in the elevator and pressed the bell at number H.719. Dick made me do the talking when we were greeted by a huge

Chinese gent, who told us to come in and wait. We sat down in a small room while he went into another room. There were plenty of girlie books to read, but Dick and myself wanted the real thing.

We waited impatiently for about five minutes; then the door opened and out came five beauties accompanied by their huge bodyguard. We both stood up, mouths wide open – just staring! The man asked us to choose and told us how much it was for each girl and how long we could have.

I'm sure I picked the prettiest one there and she cost me twenty pounds for three hours; which I thought was long enough. We both paid the man our fees and were led away like little lambs to the slaughter. Mine took me into her bedroom, which was very posh. Her name was Vanessa and she was Portuguese. She was the only non-Chinese girl there and was about twenty-six. She turned on the shower and put the lights down low.

She then undressed me and took her own clothes off; I just stared, she had a perfect body. She was about the same height as me and had long black hair, a beautiful golden tan with boobs which were neither too big nor too small. She also had very large nipples and her mass of pubic hair was dark and soft. We both went into the shower where she washed me all over. Being young and inexperienced, I didn't touch her once in the shower. She just smiled and dried me off.

The night was cool, so there was no need to put the electric fan on in the room. We lay down on top of her giant-sized bed and she just led me all the way. There was nothing she couldn't do for a man. It was one of the best times I've ever experienced. Soon my three hours were up and like Dick in the other room I didn't want to leave. We did however, and we didn't say a word to each other going down in the elevator. But when we got outside the noise of the traffic brought us out of our trance and we didn't stop talking. We agreed how great they were, well worth the money. We went back into the Paradise Bar and happily got drunk.

I suppose being drunk makes seamen do silly things, such as having tattoos done. Dick and myself, accompanied by a few others, made for Pinkies, the famous Hong Kong tattooist. I had already had one done when I was at home, so I thought one more wouldn't hurt. Dick was more sensible and decided not to have any done, but Billy Stewart, a Welshman, had two big eyes tattooed on his arse. It took all of us to hold him down, but he persevered. I was going to have the eyes also but chickened out and decided on a little motto which reads, 'The sweetest girl I've ever seen kissed was another man's wife – my mother!'

By this time I was well under and felt bad, so Dick and myself caught a taxi back to the ship, where we both crashed out until we were called the following morning. That morning we left Hong Kong. I felt a bit sad, but you always do when you get attached to some place you like. We left Hong Kong on 4th February, 1975. It was raining and miserable and I shed a few tears. Our next port of call was Shimonoseki in Japan.

*

The propellers were turning and we were on our way to Japan accompanied by HMS *Leander*, a frigate, on which an uncle of mine, Brian Bourke, had sailed. That evening, out in the rough and stormy Chinese sea, a film was being shown in the crew mess. It was a James Bond movie, and it started off in Hong Kong harbour; as soon as we saw that, we all cheered.

It was a very rough journey which took us three days, and it was on the morning of 7th February, that we first caught sight of Moji Bridge. Moji is on the northern part of the South island, and Shimonoseki was the other side of the bridge on the main island.

It was snowing heavily when we docked, but the snow didn't stop the people of Shimonoseki from giving us a welcoming party. Many children waved little Japanese and British flags. The small town was covered by at least six inches of snow and it was bitterly cold, but our hosts still managed a little smile, despite the cold weather.

As our visit was only for three days, we had to cram as many things in as possible. So, that afternoon, the mayor of Shimonoseki and many other well-to-do people came on board for lunch. By this time I was no longer in the pantry washing dishes, but serving in the saloon, wearing my white shirt, bow tie, and blue trousers. I felt ready to serve the Queen. The mayor brought along three of his maids to help us with the serving. It wasn't a fancy meal, just a plain four-course dinner with rice pudding as dessert, followed by cheese and coffee. Anyway, they all seemed to enjoy it and after proposing a toast to the Queen, they all left for the bar.

That evening I went ashore with Billy Witts. The snow was deep and it was very cold. We walked along a narrow street, with small cars and motorbikes tearing back and forth. The people were all very small and stared at us as if we were some beings from another planet. I noticed a cake shop which was still open, so I crossed the street and went inside. The cakes in the shop looked similar to those back home. I pointed to a cake which looked like a cream doughnut. The little old lady serving behind the counter couldn't understand English and I couldn't understand Japanese; the doughnut cost me two hundred yen, which is about twenty-five pence. When I got outside I looked at my cream doughnut which smelt somewhat peculiar. Nevertheless I took a bite but quickly spat it out. It was revolting. The cream was some kind of sturgeon and the cake itself was made of rice. I passed a waste-paper bin and quickly disposed of my cream doughnut.

We walked around the quiet town, which by now was under very heavy snow. So Billy and I made for the nearest bar. Inside the bar, we brushed off the snow and took our coats off; it was a small place and very quiet. There was one woman behind a small counter serving two customers. Billy asked for a beer, but the woman didn't understand. Luckily enough, one of her customers could speak a little English and explained to us that the place we were in was known as a Sake house, so we ordered some Sake which is drunk warm, from small wooden bowls. We got very chatty and the Sake soon went to our heads. That is when I exchanged a keyring for a small Sake bowl.

The snow had stopped falling outside, and as it was getting quite late Billy and I said goodbye and staggered back to the ship. The following day we had a party for all the orphaned children in Shimonoseki – about fifteen in all. It was held in the crew's messroom. There were jelly trifles, sandwiches, cakes, lemonade, and all kinds of things that kids like; but these children had never seen food quite like this before. We sat them all down and they began their feast, but the poor little devils didn't know where to begin. After the messy ordeal, each boy and girl received a present, which the crew members had subscribed for. The boys and girls had to say their names. Then they walked up to the chief engineer's wife and received their gifts. They said thank you and went outside to the gangway, ready to board a bus which was to take them back to their school.

The cold prevented me from going ashore that night, and I felt a bit tired, so I turned in early. I was up bright and early the next morning and so was the mess man, still clearing away after the kids party. Just before the ship sailed, the people of Shimonoseki were led along the street by the local brass band. It was a lovely sight as they all lined along the quay-side, waving their little flags. I went back inside the ship to my cabin to find some kind of souvenir. I took a large carving of an African elephant which I had bought in Kenya and made my way outside. I only had a light T-shirt on and soon felt the cold. As I made my way down the gangway, a little girl was smiling up at me, waving a small Japanese flag. She must have been only about five years old, so I gave her my African elephant in exchange for her little Japanese flag. I picked her up and kissed her on the cheek and went back on board. A few of the lads exchanged gifts on the quay with the locals before we sailed. The citizens waved to us as the tugboats towed us out into the harbour; and soon we were on our way to Sasebo, which is about five hundred miles south of Shimonoseki.

Chapter Six

Sasebo was an American base, so we had to get two currencies from the purser. It was quite a smooth trip down to Sasebo, but it was still very cold. Our stay there was very different to that in Shimonoseki; Sasebo was a typical American place. We were there for just over a week, and from the word go I never once stopped going ashore in the afternoons. We went to the big American stores where they sold everything. The very first day there, I bought a pocket camera and a Japanese tea set – a gift for my mother. I also played on the gaming machines and won quite a few times.

During the evenings, we spent most of our time at the American Servicemen's Club, but we soon found our way down town to the bars of Sasebo, and one night I found myself in the local sauna and massage parlour, where the girl attendant covered herself in soap suds and rolled all over me. It was quite nice, but it was a bit painful, especially below the abdomen.

On about the fifth day in Sasebo, a small number of the crew went on a trip to a Japanese tea party and I headed the queue. The party took place in a temple with lots of Geisha girls. We all removed our shoes and went inside, where we were greeted by three priests. We sat down on small mats and each one of us had at least three Geisha girls waiting on us.

We started off by drinking some kind of seaweed soup, then there was fish, rice balls, a sponge cake, which was delicious, and, of course, the famous Sake. It was a quick ceremony, a few prayers were read and then we left the temple and went outside to put our shoes on. We went out into the cold and windy weather of Sasebo. The Geisha girls were all in a long line along the path, bowing and saying farewell before we boarded the bus. I took one more glance at the last girl and smiled. She was a cracker – she just looked like a doll. We then boarded the bus and went back to the ship.

On the last night in Sasebo, most of us went to the American Servicemen's Club, I went inside to have a meal with Mickey Mouse, one of the deckhands. None of your Japanese food for us – not like the other day.

After having a huge steak, we were both bloated out, and Mick was very homesick. He asked me if I knew the standard prices of phone calls to the UK. I guessed a price and he looked in his wallet; then he went to the telephone booth. I followed and told him not to bother, but it was no good. He phoned his mother's house in Devon and was only on the phone for about five minutes, but it cost him nearly twenty pounds. He didn't want to put the receiver down, and the poor lad had tears in his eyes when he said goodbye to his mother. I tried to comfort him by telling him that he'd soon be home and he managed to pull himself together. Then he went and had a few drinks before going back to the ship.

We sailed out of Sasebo the following day; I took a few snapshots of the place before leaving. It started to snow as we left. I stood on deck as the ship steamed away once again. We were to be at sea for a full month before we'd see land again. But for some of us that night a message came through to the ship's radio room it read as follows.

Captain RFA *Green Rover*. Two of your crew members, A. Barrett and K. Bourke, who were both assaulted in Singapore on 23rd December, 1974, have been asked to attend court martial as witnesses, also J. Gillespie of HMS *Leander*, in Singapore on 5th March, 1975, for hearings of the case.

RFA *Green Rover* to rendezvous with HMS *Leander* 1200 hrs. 23rd February, 1975. HMS *Leander* to take witnesses into Manila Bay, Philippines, 24th February, 1975, HMS *Leander* to transfer witnesses on board HMS *Diomede*, HMS *Diomede* leaves Manila Bay, Philippines, 25th February, 1975, arrival in Somberwang, Singapore, 3rd March, 1975.

Witnesses will be met by officials: end of message.
Colonel-in-Command,
3rd Corps Infantry,
New Zealand Army, Nee Soon Barracks, Neo Soon, Singapore.

We were told of the message the following day. By this time the ship was at full steam ahead so that it could rendezvous with the *Leander*. The ship was due back in Singapore around April, so that meant that Barrett and myself would have nearly a two month holiday, which sounded very exciting. Then I asked the purser about the money situation. He told me that as I was still signed on the ship's articles, I'd still be paid. He also told me that I'd receive an allowance while staying in Singapore.

February 23rd soon came, and with our bags packed and our pockets bulging with Singapore dollars we left the Green Rover on the ship's crash boat. I had my camera in my hand taking shots of the ship at different angles. We soon boarded the *Leander* and she was off for Manila.

We stood on deck and watched the small tanker slowly fade away. I felt on top of the world. I thought, what a trip this has turned out to be: I'm away to work and here I am going on a two month holiday in Singapore. A young seaman carried our bags down to the petty officer's mess.

He must have thought we were something high and mighty. We were given bunks and blankets and made at home – all for one night.

The mess was quite cramped, but in no way as bad as the seaman's quarters. So here I was on board my Uncle Brian's old ship! The petty officers had a small bar in their mess, so Barrett and myself didn't get a wink's sleep that night. When we finally did crash out, it must have been about six the following morning. We were awakened at ten o'clock, as the ship had berthed in Manila, and it was time for us to depart and join our next vessel. We said cheerio to the boys in the mess and left. After being down below for nearly twenty hours, the sunlight was very strong. It was a very warm day – in fact, it was shirtsleeve weather; and to think, five days before, in Japan, it was below freezing point and snowing!

We left the *Leander* with John Gillespie, who was the other witness, and boarded the *Diomede* which was berthed just in front of the *Leander*. We went below, and again a young seaman carried our bags to the petty officers mess, while poor old Gillespie had to make do with what he was used to, the seamen's quarters. Again, we were given a bunk each and some blankets although we didn't really need them, it was so warm.

As the ship was not leaving for Singapore until the next day, Barrett, Gillespie and myself made the best of our one night fling in Manila. It was still only midday so we had all the time in the world. We caught a taxi to the main drag and went from there. We went from bar to bar, disco to disco and then Barrett brought up the subject of women. He wasn't the only one to feel that way, so we went to a sauna and massage parlour. Someone on board advised us to go to the one just off the main drag. It was supposed to be the best in town, but it wasn't the cheapest. As far as we were concerned though, it didn't matter, as Manila was the cheapest place we had been to.

We went inside the parlour and I must say it wasn't the nicest place of all, but we made do. The girls there undressed us and put us in the showers; then I was led away to a small wooden cubicle where the girl lay me down on a bench and massaged oil into my skin. I was told by the chap on board to ask for a special massage so I did. You should have seen the girl's face when I said that! She looked over her shoulder in case anyone was peeping. I wouldn't have minded, but there was a door on the cubicle and no one could see in. Then she did it; yep, she gave me the *special massage* and all that was, was a quick shake of her wrist.

'Is that all I get?' I said.

She didn't answer. All she said was 'Finished,' so I dressed and went downstairs, and I saw two long gloomy faces on Barrett and Gillespie. Obviously, they too had asked for a special massage, and both of them were disgusted, so we paid our fee and left.

When we got outside, Barrett started howling and protesting. 'A special massage indeed! Bullshit! I could have done it better myself.'

The streets were dead and everywhere was shut. It was still only ten in the evening. We walked about for fifteen minutes, trying to find somewhere to eat, but everywhere was closed. It was like a ghost town. Then all of a sudden, four Philippine soldiers jumped out in front of us, with bloody great guns. I thought we were goners. They told us to move and took us to the local police station. There we were, arms raised high in the air, and we didn't even know what we had done.

They locked us in a huge cell all on our own. Apparently, that night in Manila, they had staged a curfew which commenced at nine-thirty. They didn't ill treat us. We told them that we had only arrived that day and didn't know a thing about any curfew. They were very considerate and understood but it was their job to arrest anyone out after nine-thirty. They even fed us, as we were all starving hungry, and the following morning at six they took us back to the ship, where I went straight to my bunk and crashed out, as I had not gotten any sleep the night before.

When I woke, it was about three in the afternoon, and the ship by now was well out to sea. At five o'clock, Barrett woke, just in time for dinner, which wasn't too appetising. For our whole week on the *Diomede* all we did was sleep, eat and drink; and as there weren't any portholes, we didn't know what time of day it was. Halfway through our little trip to Singapore, the ship stopped and had a kind of sports day on the flight deck. You could also go swimming over the side, but I didn't fancy that, as the waters there were shark-infested. I ended up playing for the PO team in deck hockey which is very tough, especially on the shins.

The rest of the trip was spent down below, just lounging around. The day before arriving in Singapore, I celebrated my seventeenth birthday by drinking too much. Gillespie came into the petty officers mess as a guest, but he had to leave when it was time for lights out, which only affected the seamen's quarters.

I woke early that morning, just as the ship berthed in Somberwang. I woke Barrett, and we got our things together and left the *Diomede* along with Gillespie. On the gangway was an Indian gentleman with a white turban on his head. He asked if we were Barrett and Bourke. We said we were.

'My name is Singh,' he said, 'and I'm the RFA agent in Singapore; please will you follow me.' Awaiting us on the road was a chauffeur-driven limousine; but, again, no Gillespie, he had a military policeman waiting for him in an old jeep which took him up to 'Terror Barracks'.

The limousine took us to Singh's office, and we went

inside. I think the temperature that day was well into the nineties, but Singh's office was air-conditioned. For some reason he was treated like a king. We sat down and he told us about the allowance we would get. He said that we would be picked up every Thursday morning just before lunch.

'You'll be taken from the place at which you will stay to the paymaster's office in Somberwang. You will come under category B, which is an allowance of sixty dollars a day, that is ten pounds. You will start your allowance tomorrow, as I'm sure you haven't brought much with you. So I'll pick you up tomorrow for the paymaster's office. You will stay at Agnes Western's Mission for seamen, and I'll pick you up at ten o'clock on Friday the fifth to take you to Nee Soon Barracks for the hearings.'

Both Barrett and myself were astonished.

'You don't get so well looked after at a Butlin's holiday camp,' said Barrett – another one of his jokes.

'Oh, and before you go, I'll have four men keeping watch over you. You're quite free to travel about as much as you like on the island, but get used to being followed. It's for your own good, and as you're still here, I might as well take you to see your new bodyguards.'

We left the office and walked down a long corridor until we came to a door which had a sign saying 'Private'. Inside sat four men. Singh introduced us to them.

'This is Tony Barrett and Kevin Bourke, and they are the two new arrivals, whom you four will, I hope, keep an eye on.'

The four big men were all service men stationed in Singapore. They were Jim Sortmarsh, Paul Antrim, Gordon Jenkins and Dave Sutton; quite a tough-looking bunch!

'Now, these men will keep an eye on you most of the time, so that no harm comes to you.'

We both said cheerio and left with Singh.

I said, 'Why do we need them blokes to watch over us?'

'Well,' said Singh, 'the men who assaulted you haven't been locked up and they're got many friends; they'll probably find out where you are staying. They won't do anything personally, but their friends will have a go at trying to harm you in some way; now we don't want that to happen, do we?'

'Oh no,' said Barrett, 'my nose and jaw still haven't really healed.'

We climbed back into the limousine and drove to our new home. It was a lovely hotel, and had everything: air-conditioning, snooker rooms, tennis courts, restaurants and a swimming pool! We signed in and Singh said he would see us the next day at about eleven. Then he left, and a porter carried our bags up to our rooms. We had our own veranda, shower, toilet and a giant sized bed. The rooms were next to each other and were very similar.

We got settled in that evening, and had an early night knowing we were as safe as houses, with four bodyguards watching over us. All of a sudden I felt like someone important, and I fell asleep. The following morning I woke early. I put my shorts on and went for a swim in the hotel pool, and afterwards I joined Barrett for breakfast.

It had just gone eleven when Singh's chauffeur-driven car came to take us to the paymaster's office, which was about five minutes away by car. Of course, we received our week's money in dollars, which was a lot – four hundred and twenty to be precise, and as the hotel was quite cheap, we paid two weeks in advance. Then came the problem of finding things to do. We both wanted to see most of the island, so that afternoon in Somberwang, Barrett, who had a driving licence, hired a car. We both chipped in to hire the car for a week. It wasn't a brand-new car, it was about five years old, a French Renault, but we didn't have to bother about taxis anymore.

So off we went down the Somberwang road and back to the hotel where we got cleaned up. There were stewards who cleaned our rooms and offered to do our washing for a small wage. I became very friendly with one of the waitresses, a little Indian girl called Lily. Every time I went into the restaurant, she would drop everything just to serve me. Lily was a bit younger than me and could never pronounce my first name. I kept telling her that it was Kevin, but she insisted on saying Kelvin.

The climate in Singapore is hot nearly all the year round, as it's only forty miles north of the equator and at seven in the morning it can sometimes be as hot as one hundred degrees; the sweat just rolls off. So I used to shower at least four times a day, which meant four sets of clothing. I'm not quite sure if it happened all the year round, but it seemed that wherever we were in Singapore, in the afternoon between two and five, there was always heavy rainfall.

That evening, Barrett felt like showing off his 'new' Renault, so we set off for 'Terror Barracks', where Gillespie was staying. We were closely followed by Sortmarsh and Jenkins in a blue Hillman. Barrett felt like playing car chase, but decided on just playing it cool. We picked up Gillespie who had been bored all day, and made our way into Singapore City. We ventured on foot around Chinatown, closely observed by our bodyguards. Barrett couldn't drink much as he was driving. We had a quick snack at Fatty's and went and saw a movie, which was all about a ship that was hit by a tidal wave and was turned right over.

We had to make it an early night that evening, as the court hearing was to be the following day. I felt sorry for Gillespie as we dropped him off, for he was made to work for his money, while Barrett and myself could do as we pleased. Early the next day we were taken to Nee Soon Barracks for the court hearing, which was all very boring.

They kept us hanging around for hours. We had to identify the two defendants – a Private Williams and a Private Godfrey. Williams was well over six foot and would match Mohammed Ali in weight. He was the one who assaulted me, and poor old Barrett still remembered Godfrey.

We had lunch in the camp's dining hall before returning to more boring waiting. Singh told us that it would be all over in an hour, and there we were three hours later. It was about three-thirty when it came to an end. The defendants were marched out and an army sergeant came over to us and told us that it was all over until the court martial three weeks later. The Sergeant's name was Daniels, the sort of chap who wanted Williams and Godfrey put behind bars.

'It's not the first time,' he said. 'That bloody pair are always in some brawl and this time, I want to get them.' He told us about their not being locked up. 'The court martial is in three weeks' time, and all the Colonel in Command has done is to give them extra duties. I mean, he hasn't even confined them to camp. They can do what they like, when they like and how they like – diabolical, I reckon.' He told us to watch out for them, and then left.

Singh had been waiting outside for the past hour and was looking fed up when we emerged.

Back at the hotel, it meant just lazing around and enjoying ourselves. Singh told us he'd be in touch. That weekend we stayed in, mainly around the bar and the swimming pool, and talked to Lily, but on the Sunday, after taking an early morning swim, I started to sunbathe, and ended up in agony. I must have stayed in the sun for a bit too long, and I soon started to fry.

For the next few days, I hardly saw Barrett as I was confined to bed with blisters the size of golf balls all over my back. By the Thursday, I made sure I was okay so that I could go and pick up my allowance. Barrett became very friendly with a Chinese girl called Maureen, who lived in

Nee Soon, so on the Friday, Barrett, Maureen and I set off for Tiger Balm Gardens which were right on the other side of the Island.

Before going into the city, we went into Somberwang to pay another week's rent on the car. On our way to the gardens, we stopped off at Lions City, where there was a huge shopping centre. We were mainly interested in the stereo equipment store, but Maureen being a native, told us she could get us good sets for half the price, so we skipped the stores and drove on to the gardens.

The gardens were spectacular, all very colourful. I had brought my camera along and took many shots. There were numerous statues in the gardens, mainly of animals, and quite a few of the god Buddha, with his big smiling face and large belly. Barrett was very interested in the stereos that Maureen knew of, so on our way back to the hotel, we stopped off at Nee Soon, where Maureen knew a man who dealt in stereos.

'He gets them straight from the warehouses,' she said.

We went into his shop where he greeted Maureen. She introduced us to him. His name was Danny Tuck. He showed us many models and new styles which had just arrived from Japan. Those he was selling were almost half the price of those in the city and a quarter of the price they would be in the UK. Barrett chose a model. He also bought a few cassettes. Danny didn't ask for the money straight-away – just a down payment. I also bought a set but not as large as the one Barrett bought.

That afternoon, Danny fixed both sets up in our hotel rooms, and that night we went up to Bugis Street for a drink; we left the car and went by taxi. That was the night I was glad to have a couple of heavies watching over me. It was about midnight when our little encounter occurred. The street was packed out with ladyboys. Then I noticed Williams and a few other lads, all pretty drunk. He soon noticed me and he stormed over to our table. Then he stopped just like a bull. He was massive. He ignored Barrett and looked straight at me. I was shaking with fear, wondering what he'd do.

'So you're the little bastard who might put me away.'

He looked very mean. I was going to look behind to where Antrim and Jenkins were sitting, but didn't. Barrett stayed silent.

So did I for a while, and then I said, 'Yep, that's right, big boy. I'm going to put you away where you belong – caged up with all the other monkeys in the zoo.'

At this, Barrett left the table laughing and, to my surprise so did Williams – then I started laughing myself. Barrett soon came back.

'You know,' he said, 'I've got to hand it to you. You bloody stand up for yourself.'

'I only said that because I knew our bodyguards were behind us.' I looked behind me, expecting Antrim and Jenkins to be there, but they had left about fifteen minutes before!

Up to the time that we went to the court martial itself, we usually hung around the hotel. We often saw Maureen and Danny. We also saw Singh on our allowance days which we always looked forward to. On 21st March, a ship came in to Somberwang, so Barrett, Gillespie and myself went aboard. In the crew bar that night there was a darts tournament being held, and as we were visitors and didn't know anyone, we made our own team. There were about ten teams in all; but we showed them how to play! We slowly went through each round successfully, and soon reached the final, where we met three army lads, and were to play the best out of five games.

They soon went two games up, but we came back to level the score, so it was all on the last game. They were left with one hundred and four, but Gillespie left me double sixteen. Then it was their throw, treble twenty and four. Then all that was left was double tops. I turned away, thinking he would get it, but he missed, so it was all up to me. I took aim at the double sixteen and threw. It went straight in and we had won. Each of us received a small winner's plaque.

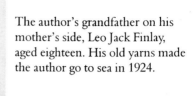

The author's grandfather on his mother's side, Leo Jack Finlay, aged eighteen. His old yarns made the author go to sea in 1924.

New Year's Eve 1974–75, in Ships Company at a bar in Bugis Street known also as Boogie Street, Singapore.
From left to right: Prout, Witts, Scotch Pete, 'The Postman', an uncertified deck hand, the author, and Davey Belt.

The author as a steward on *Green Rover*, April 1975. This photograph was taken a day after the author had his head shaved by the rest of the crew.

The crew bar known as 'The Pig'(and Whistle). The author is second from left and Tony Barret second from right, with two other crew members who were all on the same court marshall 'Channels Night' – the night before docking in the UK. They had been away for nine months.

The author as he is today, on the North Sea, 1997; as the Cook Steward in the gallery on the MV *Sand Serin*.

Chapter Seven

The day soon came for the court martial, and Singh arrived on time. I was very nervous as we drove slowly along the road. We entered the barracks and the car stopped outside a group of offices where, standing to attention in uniform, were Williams and Godfrey. We went inside to a small waiting room, where Gillespie and Sergeant Daniels were seated.

'Oh good,' said Daniels, 'I'm glad you're here, now maybe I can go over a few things before I have to go inside the court room.'

He told us that Gillespie would go in first; then Barrett and then me. I asked him how long it would take. He said that he didn't know. We all had to go into the court room to be sworn in. On the bench sat six very high-ranking officers, and in front of them sat two typists. To their left were Williams and Godfrey, who were heavily guarded. Then we went back into the small waiting room.

About five minutes later, Gillespie was called for. He was wearing his white tropical naval uniform; you could hear him come to attention. He was only in there for about ten minutes. When he came back into the waiting room, Barrett was called for. I asked Gillespie what they had asked him. He told me he said just what had happened to him on the night of 23rd December, 1974. Barrett was in there for a bit longer. The nerves were now creeping upon me. Then they called for me. I stood up timidly and went inside. I was directed to sit down just in front of the typists and was told to speak clearly and not too fast.

There was a New Zealand naval officer sitting beside Williams and Godfrey, and Sergeant Daniels was seated to my left. An army corporal approached me with a Bible in his hand. He told me to hold the Bible and he said, 'Do you swear to tell the truth, the whole truth, and nothing but the truth. So help you God?' I said 'Yes,' but was told to say, 'I do.'

Then the questions started. I was asked my name, religion and occupation. Then what I did on the night of 23rd December, 1974, and who I was with. I was asked if the person who assaulted me was in the room. I said that he was and I had to point him out. So I pointed to Williams.

It turned out to be a long and tiring day. Eventually the court adjourned for lunch. After lunch we were made to sit in the waiting room nearly all the afternoon. Then Daniels came in and told us that they had adjourned for a recess. He told us what had been happening and he reckoned that there was no way Williams and Godfrey would get off. Then he went back into the court room.

About an hour later, all three of us were called, we went into the court room to hear the verdict. Both Williams and Godfrey stood in front of the officers, and the general in the centre spoke.

'You have both been in trouble before and have been let off lightly; but not this time. You're behaviour was disgraceful and we have all come to a decision. Private Errol Godfrey we find you guilty on the grounds of assault on Anthony Barrett, breaking his nose and jaw. This court sentences you to eighteen months' detention and then dismissal from the army; Private Robert Williams, you have been found guilty on the grounds of assault on Kevin Bourke and carrying a knife, which you used on John Gillespie. The knife you carried was a lethal weapon and John Gillespie suffered many injuries as the result of losing a great amount of blood. We have to punish you severely, and this court sentences you to three years' detention and then dismissal from the army.'

I couldn't believe it, and neither could Williams. He was in tears as they were 'doubled' away. Later, outside, Daniels, too, looked shocked. He didn't think Williams would get as long as that. I felt a sudden rush of sorrow for Williams. I asked Daniels where they would go. He told me that they would be flown back to New Zealand that night. Singh arrived and we said goodbye and left.

I looked at Barrett, who was quiet. 'I didn't think he would get such a long time in detention.'

'No,' said Barrett, 'neither did I.'

We weren't needed any longer, so we spent the rest of our stay just lounging around, waiting for the ship to come back. About three days after the shock of the court martial, Danny came to take us into town for a massage. He knew of a place which the likes of us would never find. His friend ran the parlour and was very pleased to see Danny. We didn't go to his parlour but to his home where Danny told him what we wanted. So he made a quick phone call and in five minutes there were three Chinese beauties knocking at his door. We chose a girl each and went upstairs. The bedrooms in his house had everything, and the girl I had was quite nice. I never caught her name, but whoever she was, she soon had me down to my birthday suit. I had a great time with her. Usually I pick the small girls, but not this time. She was very tall and thin, but she sure knew how to get down to business. Danny knew the chap in charge, so we got it dead cheap – about twenty dollars each, which is just over three pounds.

The following day was the day I was really fed up. So, like a fool, I wrote a letter to the Queen, you know, the one who lives in Buckingham Palace. I made out in the letter that I was a young innocent kid, who had just started at sea.

I told her that I had been beaten up and was made to go to the court martial, and that I was in Singapore alone and not getting much money to live on. I wrote that I was badly treated by the officials and that I longed for my mother. I made it a right tearful letter. I signed the letter and put the ship's address at the top. I addressed it to Her Majesty, Queen Elizabeth II, Buckingham Palace, London, SW, England. I put three first class stamps on the envelope, and at the top I wrote the word 'Urgent' and underlined it.

Although our stay in Singapore was delightful, we were glad to get away. At last, on 8th April, the *Green Rover* docked in Somberwang, and Barrett and I packed our bags, put our stereo equipment back in the boxes and put it all into the car. We said goodbye to the staff and thanked them for putting up with us. Little Lily was in tears as we were going. I told her I'd come up and say goodbye before the ship left. She asked for a picture of me, so I gave her a recent close-up of my ugly mug and asked for one of her. I needn't have bothered, as she modestly gave me one. I gave her a little kiss on the cheek and said goodbye.

We had a lot of luggage as we set off for the docks. We were both looking forward to getting back on board. We parked just by the gangway and started carrying our gear aboard. It seemed as though we had been away for ages. A lot of the lads had grown beards and their hair had grown longer. Mind you, I could have done with a haircut too. Dick helped me carry my gear on board; it was nice to be back. Mike Bartley was glad to have me back. We had only been away for seven weeks, but it seemed like seven months. As they were short of staff, I worked that afternoon, and Barrett took the car back.

After work that evening, I put most of my gear away and rigged up my brand new stereo, which was now paid for, thanks to that allowance. That night I stayed on board and was going to have an early night, but ended up drinking in the bar. The ship was due to stay in Somberwang for a week before leaving for Ceylon.

The following day, when I was ashore, accompanied by several big deckhands, having a haircut – well, it was more like a crew-cut as I had no hair when the barber finished – John, the messman, told me to hurry back to the ship because it was sailing in half an hour. Most of us were ashore that day, so we all rushed back to the ship not knowing what was happening. Everyone was present when the ship sailed and no one knew where we were going.

Then over the tannoy, the captain spoke. He told us that we were going up to Saigon in Vietnam, where the Americans had pulled out; the Vietcong were moving into Saigon fast and many refugees were trying to leave the country. The ship was soon steaming at twenty knots, and as we were going into dangerous waters, our pay trebled; but the money didn't bother me; I just hoped that there wasn't going to be any trouble.

⋆

The following evening we anchored off Saigon. We were about thirty miles offshore. The whole sky was lit up. It was like a gigantic bonfire night. There were many other ships anchored off that night. The next day, we saw many small boats, packed with South Vietnamese refugees; they were trying to make their way to Thailand. There were many fleeing refugees, but we never picked any up and we never went back to Singapore. So I didn't say my final goodbye to Lily and our visit to Ceylon was cancelled. There was a rumour going around that we might go to Brazil in South America.

We were soon on our way and we were going to Brazil; we weren't quite sure where to; it was either Santos, Salvador or Rio de Janeiro! Most of us were hoping for Rio.

We were in a group of ships all travelling at a moderate speed going south into the Indian ocean and saying farewell to the Orient. On our way out to Brazil we were to call in on one of the islands in the Indian Ocean – a small well-known island, called Mauritius.

★

We arrived in Port Louis, Mauritius on 21st April, 1975. Mauritius had all the right things for a swell holiday. There was the deep blue sea, with miles of golden sand and coconut trees. On that day two big bags of mail arrived on board. There were two letters addressed to me: one from my mother asking how I was, and another which had the crown and ER stamped on its envelope. It was my reply from the Queen. I quickly opened the letter, and on a small white piece of paper was the Royal Coat of Arms, with the words 'Buckingham Palace' directly below it. The letter read:

> The Defence Services Secretary is commanded by Her Majesty the Queen to acknowledge the receipt of Mr Kevin Bourke's letter, which has been passed to the Ministry of Defence for attention.

There was no signature of any kind, just the date, 25th March, 1975. I was soon showing off the letter to everyone on board, and Mike Bartley, the purser, found it amusing, and asked if he could borrow it so that he could show it to all the officers. By the following day, with my by now, very popular letter, I was the talk of the ship, especially amongst the three lady passengers. I think the only one who didn't know was the captain himself.

That evening, we all went ashore. We started off at the Seamen's Mission, where I sent home a few postcards. The main attraction in Mauritius was the Silver Moon Club, which was a taxi ride from the Mission. The currency there is rupees and the chief spoken language is French. Most of the ship's crew made for the Silver Moon which, of course, was a right dive. There were girls of all shapes and sizes, and cockroaches running wild all over the floor – but it was fun. I think we were all happy, because we were going home – we drank and danced until we almost dropped.

The club closed at midnight, and behind it was the local brothel. Each one of us had some kind of girl to go around with. I ended up by going with a girl who had skinny legs and was wearing a mini-skirt. She looked a right mess, but she was one of the best the club had to offer.

Inside the caged brothel, we all paid for the girls and the room. That very day, on arriving in Mauritius, the second mate, Bob Ferguson, had told us of the high rate of vene-real disease and had asked us to take some contraceptives with us; but most of us were too drunk that night to even do it, let alone try to get one of those things on. Every room in the brothel was occupied by a member of the crew of the *Green Rover*. The girl I had for the night was okay. I didn't ask her name, as I didn't really want to know. Most of us were out of the rooms by four that morning. We didn't go straight back to the ship as there was a beach by the brothel and it was very warm. So most of us went for a swim to sober up. I just dived in, fully clothed.

*

The ship was in Mauritius for two days but I didn't go ashore on the second day, and at ten o'clock on the morn-ing of 23rd April, 1975, the ship sailed, bound for Salvador in Brazil. Most of us were a bit disheartened, as we had set our minds on Rio. The ship had been at sea for two days when we went around the Cape and into bad weather.

That evening the Captain received a message from the Ministry of Defence concerning me and my letter to the Queen. The following day, he had me up in his cabin, along with Mike Bartley. He was furious and told me that when one writes to someone as high as the Queen, one must ask for his permission first. He told Mike that he would have to write a letter to the Ministry of Defence explaining what had happened; so that afternoon, Mike typed out three long letters, one for the Ministry of Defence, one to be kept by the Captain and one for me, as a souvenir.

When Mike had finished all three letters, he came to my cabin to give me my copy; I went through it quickly. It mainly stated why I wrote the letter, and that I wrote and posted it in Singapore, so that I couldn't have asked for the Captain's permission. The end of the letter was the best part. It read:

I have found Bourke a truthful youngster with a strong sense of justice. He is no troublemaker. It can be readily understood that having been transported to Singapore under uncomfortable conditions and having spent nearly two months being largely ignored and having appeared in court for only two brief periods he felt frustrated. I find Kevin Bourke to be a hard worker and one who displays a willingness to learn. It is his first trip to sea and the petition is an indication of his initiative and sense of fair play. I suspect that he will either go far or end up on the gallows.

The letter was signed James A. Bailey, Captain. I was soon showing off my new letter! I had most of the crew on their backs with laughter. The ship soon crossed the Atlantic and reached Brazil. We arrived in Salvador on 3rd May, 1975, and that day I received yet another letter, this time from the Ministry of Defence. The letter was a very nice one saying that if any British subject were ever in a situation like the one I described, he or she would be well looked after. So I might have started something after all!

It was raining heavily when we arrived in Salvador, but that didn't stop us from going ashore. Salvador was a fascinating place; the girls were beautiful and there was dancing everywhere you went. The people even danced in the supermarkets as they did their shopping. Most of us ended up just drinking and going with the girls. I did a lot of dancing in the clubs. I remember the first night; a girl started dancing all on her own – I don't think there was enough room for any one else! She was massive. She must have weighed in at about fifteen stone!

Somehow I found myself on the dance floor with her and ended up by doing the bump. I danced with her for about an hour. Then I fell on my back; she was too good for me; she didn't stop dancing all night! By the end of the evening, I ended up with a beautiful slim senorita, who couldn't speak a word of English – not many of them can – she just spoke her native language which was Portuguese.

The following day, I had the day off, so I went ashore with Dick. We did some shopping and dancing and I took my camera along and took a few shots of different places. Salvador was a very modern city; it is about a thousand miles north of Rio, but, like Rio, it has many tourists from all parts of the globe. The weather was bad; it never once stopped raining. I bought many souvenirs to take home with me. Chiefly items made of leather. I bought a South American cowboy's hat for my younger brother, Ian, and a wallet for my father.

We were in Salvador for only a week, but I went ashore every night and had a great time. I had been away from home for eight months – the longest time ever – and I was feeling very homesick. I was looking forward to getting back. We left Salvador on 10th May, 1975, and spent the next three weeks at sea, exercising with the Brazilian navy.

One of the lady passengers on board was a Mrs Shelly, who was a Royal Navy officer's wife. She had been a journalist in her younger days. To pass the time, she wanted to interview three of the ship's crew, preferably one from each department, and she started off with the catering department. She decided to pick yours truly. That evening, I accompanied Mrs Shelly to the radio room, where one of the radio officers started to tape our discussion. She asked me, amongst other things, what kind of music I liked, and she played various records. Finally, the radio officer got all the tapes together and our fifteen minute discussion was played over the ship's tannoy the next day; then she had discussions with Billy Witts from the deck department and Tony Barrett from the engine room.

★

We were now getting close to home and I was feeling very excited. After completing our exercises with the Brazilian navy, we stopped at Gibraltar, along with all the other ships which had made the long nine months voyage. We spent two days in Gibraltar, but I spent pounds on clothes, and the very first night ashore I got drunk on real British ale, which I hadn't tasted for nine months! Then I did a stupid thing: I stole a bicycle from a street corner and started riding it down a one way street. Of course, I was the one going the wrong way and I ended up smashing into a car, and would you believe it? It was police car. I spent that night in a cell! Luckily enough, I was let off lightly; they just told me not to come ashore anymore. I took no notice and went again the next night; well, it was our last night and everyone else went ashore so I joined them.

The town that night was packed out with drunken sailors, all looking forward to getting home. I arrived back on board, early the next day, just in time to start work. That day the ship sailed for home. I hardly slept for the next couple of nights and on Channel's night which was 10th June, 1975, the night before we docked at Portsmouth, we were all in the crew bar boozing. That night was also a restless night for me. I must have dozed off, but I wasn't asleep for long, when Ray Scully, the duty quarter-master, pulled both Dick and me out of our bunks.

He was well drunk and said, 'We're home boys, we're bloody home.'

'Yes, Ray, we're home; it's been a long time, but we're back now.'

About three hours later, I was standing on deck, admiring the English coastline when Mike Bartley came up to me and said, 'Do you remember, nine months ago, when we both stood here on deck and watched that same coastline fade away?'

'Yes,' I said, 'a long time ago, eh?'

'But you've seen and done a lot since then, eh Kevin? Are you glad you came?'

'Oh yeah, I'll never forget it, it's been great seeing all those places, and I'm still just a boy, really!' Over the tannoy, the local naval radio announced our arrival, after being away for nine months.

We finally docked on the Gosport side, it was a lovely day, the sun was shifting and it just felt great to be back. No one could go ashore until the customs had cleared the ship and, as it took quite a while, no one could be paid off until the following day, so that evening, everyone went ashore together, probably for the last time. I made a phone call to my parents that night telling them I'd see them the next day at my aunt's house in London. Then I joined the rest of the lads in the local pub, which was called the Ark Royal.

I was sitting with Tony Barrett and Billy Witts who were both sipping away at their pints. I was having a real good look at everyone in the pub, people I didn't know from Adam, all friendly and happy, playing darts and talking about football, proper English folk.

'Well, Kevin,' said Barrett, 'the trip wouldn't have been much without you. I've gone through agony because of you, but it was well worth it, and tomorrow it will all come to an end.'

We left the pub at closing time and made our way back to the ship for the last time. In the crew mess the next day, there was a lot of money flying around, as we all collected what money we had left on board and then signed off the articles. I said goodbye to Captain Bailey and Mike Bartley, who were both staying on board, and to most of the other lads who were staying on, and then made my way with all my luggage, to the railway station. There I left Barrett, Witts and Dick, as they were going in the opposite direction. As the train left the station I waved to a great bunch of lads.

It was a short journey, and I soon noticed Big Ben and the Houses of Parliament, and then I knew I was in London. The train pulled in at Waterloo and I stepped out on to the platform and stretched my arms. It was a hot day, 12th June, 1975. Most of my luggage was in the luggage compartment, so I grabbed hold of a trolley and made for the front of the train, where I saw a station guard heaving luggage out of the carriage. Then I noticed that he had hold of my stereo.

'Don't bloody throw that,' I said, angrily, 'that's a stereo set and it's been half-way around the world. It doesn't take too kindly to people who throw it about.' I collected my luggage and left the station.

I went through a big archway in the centre of the station, to where there was a taxi rank; I didn't have to wait too long before a taxi drew up. I told the driver where I wanted to go and piled all my luggage inside. The journey took about twenty minutes and finally I arrived. I got out of the taxi, paid the driver and took out all my belongings. I didn't have to knock at the door as they all saw me through the window and were soon outside. My mother kissed and hugged me.

'I'm glad you're home, son,' she said.

They helped me carry my luggage into the house.

'Well, are you glad you're back?' my mother said.

'Yes, it's been a long time,' I said, 'but it's nice to be home. Yep there's no place like home.'

Afterword

The author has recently joined the Merchant Navy Association, a new organisation that requires further recruits. The author, therefore, requests support for the official Merchant Navy Day on 3rd September in memory of the brave men whose grave is the sea.